The History and Archaeology of Cathedral Square Peterborough

Stephen Morris

Archaeopress Archaeology

Archaeopress Publishing Ltd
Summertown Pavilion
18-24 Middle Way
Oxford OX2 7LG

www.archaeopress.com

ISBN 978 1 78491 661 9
ISBN 978 1 78491 662 6 (e-Pdf)

© Archaeopress and the individual authors 2017

Cover: View of Cathedral Square in 2009, looking east from the tower of St John the Baptist, towards the Cathedral Gateway

All rights reserved. No part of this book may be reproduced, in any form or by any means, electronic, mechanical, photocopying or otherwise, without the prior written permission of the copyright owners.

This book is available direct from Archaeopress or from our website www.archaeopress.com

Contents

List of Figures v
List of Tables vii
Contributors ix
Acknowledgements xi

1. Introduction 1
    Background 1
    Location and topography 1
    Original objectives 3
    Methodology 3
        Fountain area excavation 3
        Detailed watching brief 3

2. Historical background 7
    Prehistory 7
    Iron Age and Roman settlement 7
    The early monastery 7
    The Danish raid, the rebuilding of the monastery and the Saxon burh 7
    The church of St John the Baptist 8
    The dissolution of the monastery 9
    John Speed's map of 1610 9
    Thomas Eyre's map of 1721 10
    The twentieth century 15

3. The Archaeology of Cathedral Square 17
    Archaeological interventions and summary chronology 17
    Anglo-Saxon activity (7th to 11th centuries) 17
        The underlying natural geology 17
        A lack of buried soil 17
        Early features 17
        Abbot Martin de Bec's 'New Town' (12th-14th centuries) 18
            The New Town 18
            Abbot de Bec's market square, 1145 18
        The Norman or West Gate of the Cathedral precinct 18
        The watercourse and the Cathedral Gateway Bridge 20
        The Chapel of St Thomas the Martyr 20
        Medieval features along Cumbergate 21
        A medieval building (Building 1) 22
        Dark organic street silts 22
    The church of St John the Baptist (15th century) 23
        The new parish church 23
        A previously unknown cemetery 24
        Church Street 25
    The post-medieval Cathedral Square (late 15th-17th centuries) 26
        Building in the south-east corner of Cathedral Square 26
        Street surfaces and paths 27
        Street monument: The market cross? 27
        Butchers Row 28
        Dark organic silts 29
    The Guildhall and the redevelopment of the square (late 17th century) 29
        The Guildhall 29
        Resurfacing of the square 30
        Churchyard pitched-stone surface 32
        Church Street pavement 34
        Queen Street 34
        Surface silts 34

  Redevelopment of Cathedral Square (late 18th early 19th centuries) 34
    Resurfacing of the square 35
    Surface silts 37
  The modern square (19th-20th centuries) 38
    Buildings between the parish church and the Guildhall 39
    The Corn Exchange 39
    Bridge Street (Narrow Bridge Street) 39
    Cumbergate 39
    Exchange Street 39
    Queen Street, 18th-century townhouse 39
    Cowgate trench 41
    Church of St John the Baptist 43
    Victorian services 43
    Development in the 20th century 46

4. The finds and environmental evidence 49
  The pottery 49
    The pottery fabrics 49
    Residuality and the industries supplying the Market Square 49
    Dating and context 49
    Key structures and deposits: 51
      Cathedral Square, Building 3 51
      The dark silts 52
  Building stone 52
    Stone mortar 52
    Architectural stone in Alwalton marble 53
      Capital 53
      Shaft 53
    Other architectural stone from the Street Monument 53
    Other architectural stone 53
      Catalogue of worked stone illustrations 53
  Stone roof tile 55
  Other finds 56
    The finds 56
    Personal possessions 58
      Buckles 59
      Lace chapes 59
      Mounts 59
      Pins 59
      Miscellaneous fittings 59
      Purse frame 60
      Recreation 60
    Building equipment 60
    Household equipment 60
      Kitchen ware 60
      Key 60
      Candle holder 61
      Vessel glass 61
    Tools 61
      Shears 61
      Thimbles 61
    Knives 61
      Whittle-tang knives 61
      Scale-tang knife 61
    Trade 61
    Horse equipment 61
    Weapons 62
      Catalogue of Illustrated finds 62

  Millstone 62
  Wood 62
  Coins 62
 Leather 64
  Methodology 64
  Late medieval footwear 64
  Sixteenth-century footwear 65
  Seventeenth-century footwear 65
  Bucket 66
  Straps 66
  Waste leather 66
  The leather from Cathedral Square in its local and regional context 66
   Catalogue of illustrated leather 67
 Ceramic building material 67
  Brick 67
  Ceramic roof tile 67
  Ceramic floor tile 69
  Mortar and plaster 70
 Clay tobacco-pipes 70
 The animal bone 70
  The animal bone assemblage 70
  Species present 71
  Ageing and sexing 71
  Pathologies 71
  Discussion 72
 Plant macrofossils 72
 Marine shells 73

5. Discussion 75
 Introduction 75
 Origins and development 75
 The market place 76
 Artefacts and trade 77
 Structures on the market place 78
  Building 3 78
  Street monument: the market cross? 79
 The graveyard 79
 Conclusions 80

Bibliography 81

List of Figures

Fig 1.1: Site location 2

Fig 1.2: Development areas 4

Fig 2.1: The Norman or West Gate to the Cathedral Precinct in 2009, prior to development, looking east 8

Fig 2.2: The Church of St John the Baptist and the Guildhall in 2009, Prior to development, looking south-west 9

Fig 2.3: John Speed's Map of Peterborough, 1610 (Peterborough Museum) 10

Fig 2.4: The Guildhall, built in 1671, looking south-west 11

Fig 2.5: Thomas Eyre's Map of Peterborough, 1721 12

Fig 2.6: Miss Frances Pears' Almshouses (now Harriet's Tearooms) on Exchange Street, looking north-east 12

Fig 2.7: The plaque dedicated by the Foeffees to Miss Frances Pears for her funding to assist the aged and infirm of the parish of Peterborough 13

Fig 2.8: The Gates Memorial, moved from Cathedral Square to Bishops Road Gardens in 1963, looking north 13

Fig 2.9: Peterborough City hall, built in the 1930s on the newly created Bridge Street, looking east 13

Fig 2.10: Cathedral Square, looking east, from the tower of the Church of St John the Baptist in 1919 (the Francis Frith collection) 14

Fig 2.11: Cathedral Square, looking east, from the tower of the Church of St John the Baptist in 2009 14

Fig 3.1: Posthole with *in situ* wooden post, at the east end of Cathedral Square 18

Fig 3.2: Survival of the 12th-century Market Square surface 19

Fig 3.3: de Bec's Market Square surface, sealed by dark silt of the 12th to 17th centuries, Cathedral Square, looking west 20

Fig 3.4: Gas trench at the cathedral west gate, showing stone foundations of the 12th to 14th centuries, looking north-east 20

Fig 3.5: Foundation of the south turret of the 14th-century west gate, partially disturbed by services of the early 20th century, looking south-east 21

Fig 3.6: Buildings at the east end of Cathedral Square 22

Fig 3.7: Medieval and post-medieval street frontages along Cumbergate 23

Fig 3.8: Dark silt over de bec's market square surface, on the north side of cathedral square 24

Fig 3.9: De Bec's market square surface, with overlying dark silt and showing later resurfacing 24

Fig 3.10: Early churchyard wall, north side of Church Street, looking north 25

Fig 3.11: Churchyard burials to the west of the church 26

Fig 3.12: The skull of burial HB1 26

Fig 3.13: The femurs of burial HB6 overlying the feet of one or two earlier burials, HB7 26

Fig 3.14: Kerb stones edging a pathway of the 15th century, against the stone churchyard wall (right), with the road (left) at a lower level, trench 6 27

Fig 3.15: The pavement surfaces in Church Street from the 12th to 20th centuries (top) and the pavements in relation to the sunken churchyard (bottom) 28

Fig 3.16: The fountain array area with the two deeper trenches containing walls and floors of Building 3, looking north-east 29

Fig 3.17: Extant stone wall of Building 3 (foreground) with robbed wall and floors behind, looking north 30

Fig 3.18: Building 3, the east wall, foreground, and narrow internal walls and floors behind, built over the levelled remains of Building 1, looking west 30

Fig 3.19: Pavement and street surface on the west side of Building 3 30

Fig 3.20: Remains of the 15th-16th-century street monument in Cathedral Square 31

Fig 3.21: Stone mortar set in the floor of building on Butchers Row, possibly to use as a urinal 31

Fig 3.22: The sexton's house, floor layers and possible urinal in section 32

Fig 3.23: Flagstones at west end of churchyard may outline the location of the sexton's house at the north end of Butchers Row, looking south towards the surviving burgage tenement buildings on church street 32

Fig 3.24: The Guildhall in 1896, looking west, showing the row of buildings between the Guildhall and the church 33

Fig 3.25: The eastern façade of the Guildhall 33

Fig 3.26: Guildhall stone foundations in fountain drain trench on the east side of the building, Guildhall to right, looking south-west 34

Fig 3.27: Pitched-stone path of the 17th century, overlaid by a pitched-stone pavement of the late 18th to early 19th century, both abutting the churchyard stone wall (right), looking west 35

Fig 3.28: Street surface of the 17th century, overlaid by the dark silt, cut by a modern pipe trench to the right, Queen Street, looking south 36

Fig 3.29: Pitched-stone surface of the late 18th- to early 19th centuries, with underlying make-up layers, sealing the dark silt under Cathedral Square in the east, looking north 36

Fig 3.30: Pitched-stone pavement with an open gutter along its outer edge, to the south of the church, cut by a Victorian brick culvert, looking east 37

Fig 3.31: Pitched-stone pavement of the 18th century, cut by a brick culvert of the 19th century, south of the church 37

Fig 3.32: Pavement at the east end of the churchyard wall, looking west 38

Fig 3.33: Buildings of the 17th century surviving on Church Street, looking south 38

Fig 3.34: Buildings between the parish church and the Guildhall 40

Fig 3.35: West of the Guildhall, a stairwell with steps down to the cellar threshold, Building 8, Cellar 4, ... 41

Fig 3.36: North-west of the Guildhall, stone cellar wall and brick floor, Building 7, Cellar 2, ... 41

Fig 3.37: Corn exchange; remains of wall and floor of the subterranean toilet, looking east 42

Fig 3.38: Miss Pears' almshouses, looking north east, with garden brick wall foundations (foreground) 42

Fig 3.39: An 18th-century town house on Queen Street, now The Grapevine public house, looking west from Exchange Street . 43

Fig 3.40: Church gateway, north-west corner of the churchyard, looking north onto Exchange Street 44

Fig 3.41: Churchyard railings on the north side of the church 44

Fig 3.42: Graffiti on 19th-century lead pipes on the church of St John the Baptist: showing a name, GRAIL, and a date of 1831 (left), and a figure in top hat and tails in a pugilist pose (right) 45

Fig 3.43: Victorian brick culvert on the north side of Church Street, cutting a pitched-stone pavement of the late 18th to early 19th century 45

Fig 3.44: Excavated section through culvert, looking north 46

Fig 3.45: Remnant granite setts of the late 19th to early 20th century, under the Cathedral's West Gate, looking south 46

Fig 3.46: Present day Cathedral Square, with the new fountain arrays in use, looking east towards the Cathedral's West Gate ... 47

Fig 4.1: Medieval mortar in Barnack limestone (SF79) 54

Fig 4.2: Octagonal capital or base in Alwalton marble (SF58) 55

Fig 4.3: Possible corbel, with a half roll 56

Fig 4.4: Part of respond/jamb (SF60) 57

Fig 4.5: Part of an octagonal moulding, possibly a step (SF59) 58

Fig 4.6: Metal finds (6-16) 63

Fig 4.7: Leather shoes (17-20) 68

Fig 4.8: Oates and Green brick (left), Halifax (right) and local Star brick (below) 69

List of Tables

Table 3.1: Summary of chronology 48

Table 4.1: Pottery fabrics 50
Table 4.2: Other finds quantified by material type 56
Table 4.3: Other finds by functional category 59
Table 4.4: Dimensions of complete bricks 69
Table 4.5: Animal bone fragmentation 71
Table 4.6: Mammals present 71
Table 4.7: Birds present 71
Table 4.8: Animal bone from dark silt sieved samples 71
Table 4.9: Tooth eruption and wear of main domesticates 72
Table 4.10: Plant macrofossils, taxa present 73

Contributors

Stephen Morris
Project Supervisor
Northamptonshire Archaeology now MOLA
(Museum of London Archaeology)

Andy Chapman BSc MCIfA FSA
Formerly Senior Archaeologist (publication),
Northamptonshire Archaeology now MOLA
(Museum of London Archaeology)

Pat Chapman BA CMS ACIfA
Formerly Project Supervisor (post-excavation)
Northamptonshire Archaeology now MOLA
(Museum of London Archaeology)

Charlotte Walker BSc ACIfA
Formerly Project Officer
Northamptonshire Archaeology now MOLA
(Museum of London Archaeology)

Iain Soden BA MCIfA
Formerly Senior Project Manager
Northamptonshire Archaeology

Jackie Hall PhD
Cathedral Archaeologist, Peterborough Cathedral
Consultant Archaeologist and Buildings Historian

Tora Hylton
Project Manager (finds and archives)
Northamptonshire Archaeology now MOLA
(Museum of London Archaeology)

Ian Meadows BA
Formerly Senior Project Manager
Northamptonshire Archaeology

Quita Mould BA MA FSA
Freelance archaeological specialist in archaeological leather of all periods

Karen Deighton MSc
Formerly Project Manager
(Environmental archaeology)
Northamptonshire Archaeology

Acknowledgements

The fieldwork was funded by Opportunity Peterborough (Peterborough City Council), through the principal contractor, Osborne. The fieldwork was monitored by Peterborough City Council Archaeological Service (PCCAS), initially the City Archaeologist, Ben Robinson, and in the later stages of fieldwork and through post-excavation by Rebecca Casa-Hatton. The Project Manager for Northamptonshire Archaeology was Adam Yates. The principal fieldworker was Stephen Morris, with assistance from Adrian Adams, James Burke, Rob Butler, Jason Clarke, Paul Clements, Nathan Flavell, David Haynes, Paul Kajewski, Laszlo Lichtenstein, Steve Porter, Rob Smith, Susan Stratton and Yvonne Wolframm-Murray. Stephen Morris has analysed the site record and prepared the report, with editing by Charlotte Walker. Pat Chapman and Andy Chapman have prepared the report for publication. The illustrations are by James Ladocha, Amir Bassir, Andy Chapman and Charlotte Walker. The client report prepared for PCCAS comprised the overview presented here, accompanied by a lengthy exposition of the full archaeological evidence, trench by trench. The client report will be available online through the Archaeology Data Service (ADS).

1. Introduction

Background

Planning permission (Ref 08/1383/R3FUL) was obtained by Opportunity Peterborough to undertake improvement works in Cathedral Square, Peterborough as part of their Public Realm Proposals. The overall site covers approximately 0.8ha and is an open public square (centred at NGR TL 1910 9865; Figs 1.1 & 2.1). The centre piece of the development was the construction of a water feature composed of two triangular fountain arrays, to the east of the 17th-century Guildhall. The other major development was the demolition of the Corn Exchange and its replacement with the new St John's Square, incorporating a stepped grassed terrace to the west of the parish church of St John the Baptist. These works were undertaken by Osborne.

The programme included new stone pavements encompassing the areas of Cathedral Square, from the Cathedral Gateway in the east to Cowgate, Queen Street and St John's Square to the west. On the north side the development extended into Cumbergate and Exchange Street, and Church Street on the south side. The enclosed yard around the parish church of St John the Baptist was also opened up. The street improvement involved the removal of the current paving slabs, the diversion of telecommunication cables and other buried utilities, the excavation of new service trenches and drainage gullies, prior to the laying of new construction materials and paving.

A cultural heritage assessment of the site identified that the development could affect archaeological remains in the area (Finch and Jones 2008). Peterborough City Council Archaeology Service (PCCAS) requested a programme of archaeological evaluation comprising the excavation of a series of archaeological test trenches.

A specification was produced by CgMs Consulting based on the brief for the proposed evaluation (Ref 10358/08/02 October 2008) which was undertaken in two phases by Northamptonshire Archaeology between November 2008 (Burke 2008) and January 2009 (in this report), from which significant archaeological remains were identified, including medieval to post-medieval stone surfaces and stone buildings. This allowed PCCAS to make informed recommendations to the local planning authority regarding the nature of archaeological mitigation for the development of the proposed fountain array, for which a brief for archaeological investigation was produced.

The core of the archaeological excavation was carried out from March to May 2009 and was centred on the trenches of the fountain array and related service trenches which were 1.0m to 1.9m below ground level. The overall development of the square was covered by a watching brief between July 2009 and August 2010, with general construction levels extending to 0.4m below current ground level. This was subject to modification in order to avoid disruption to utilities and service diversions, with deeper excavations for the new drainage and service trenches, to 2.0m deep.

The archaeological works conformed to the requirements of a specification prepared by Northamptonshire Archaeology (NA 2009) and based on the brief issued by the Peterborough City Archaeologist setting out the archaeological measures required to mitigate the impact of the development upon the archaeological resource (Robinson and Cassa-Hatton 2009).

Location and topography

The development area was centred on Cathedral Square, within the commercial centre of the city of Peterborough between the Cathedral Gateway to the east and Cowgate to the west, Church Street to the south and Exchange Street and Cumbergate to the north (Figs 1.1 and 1.2). It occupied an area of approximately 1ha, extending 200m east to west by 50m north to south. The street surfaces of the Square gently sloped down from Cowgate and Church Street in the west at 8.3m above Ordnance Datum (aOD) to the Cathedral Gateway at 7.7m aOD at the east end of the site. There was also a distinct rise in ground level from Church Street to the Queensgate entrance, Cumbergate and Exchange Street on the north of the development area at 8.8m aOD.

The Parish Church of St John the Baptist lies to the west of Cathedral Square and the Guildhall, with St John's Square (site of the former Norwich Union Building) to the west side. The north and south sides of the church are bounded by Exchange Street and Church Street respectively. The church was situated in a hollow, enclosed by a narrow, mostly level walled churchyard, set below the surrounding street level at 7.8m aOD. A clear differentiation in the street levels was visible with the churchyard 0.5m below Church Street, with at least a 1m drop from Exchange Street to the churchyard.

The underlying drift geology is believed to be river terrace deposits (sands and gravels) overlying Limestone Cornbrash based upon Oxford Clay and Kellaways Beds.

(http://www.bgs.ac.uk/geoindex/index.htm).

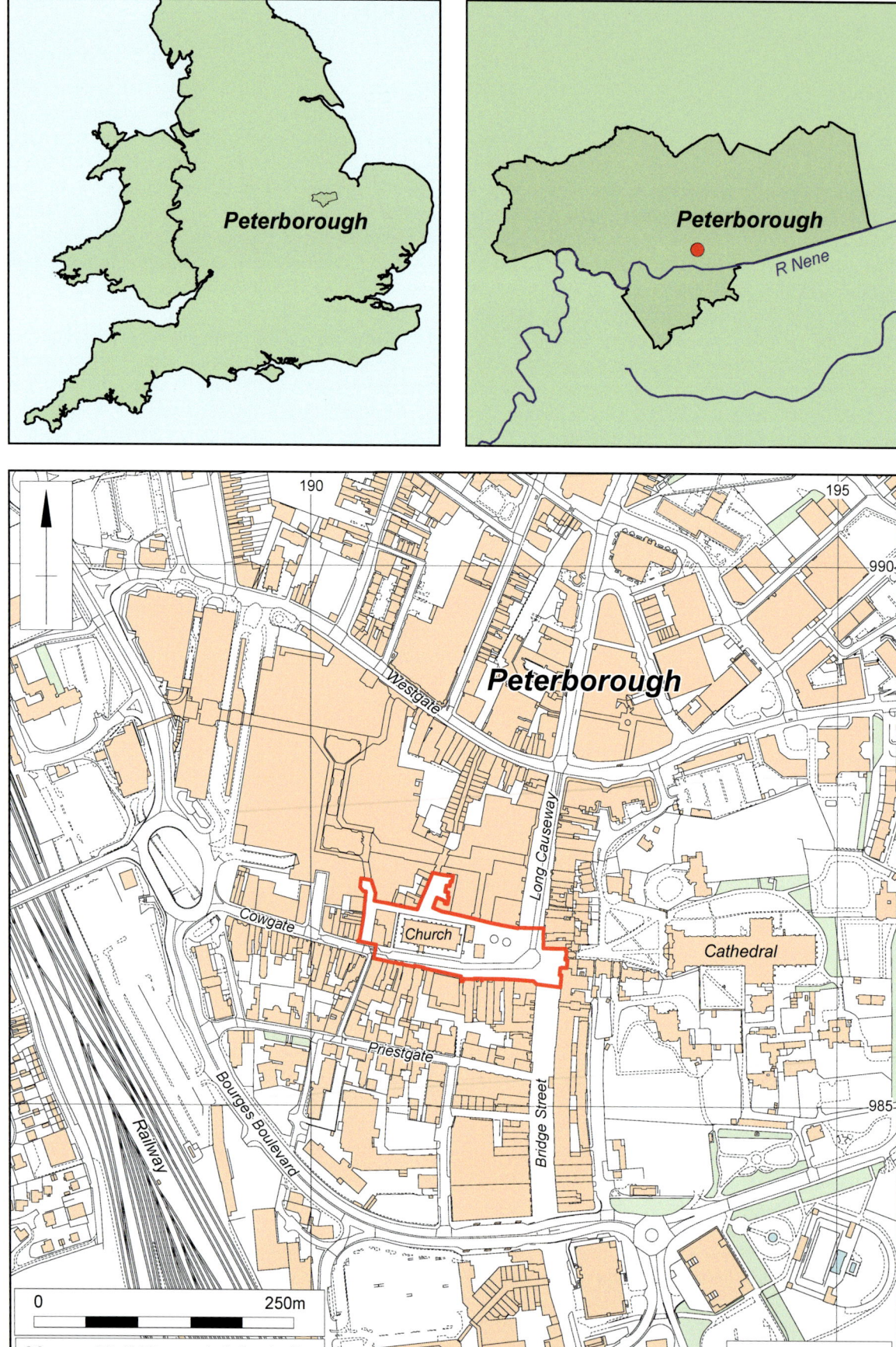

Fig 1.1: Site location

1. INTRODUCTION

Original objectives

The broad objectives were to provide detailed information regarding the date, character, extent and degree of preservation of all archaeological remains, and to define the sequence and character of activity at the site as reflected by the excavated remains; and to interpret the archaeology of the site within its local, regional, and national archaeological context.

The general investigative themes outlined by: *Research and Archaeology: A Framework for the Eastern Counties* (Glazebrook 1997; Brown & Glazebrook 2000), *Exploring Our Past* (English Heritage 1991), *English Heritage Archaeology Division Research Agenda* (1997) would also be considered.

Specifically, the investigative aims accommodated in the programme of archaeological work were to:

- Characterise and record the medieval and post-medieval market place, and street surfaces, including in-built features such as drainage gutters, decorative patterns, and partitions that relate to functional divisions;
- Analyse the construction techniques and materials used for the medieval and post-medieval market place, streets, and associated features;
- Identify record and analyse the buildings and structures that once occupied the market place. At various times covered crosses, whipping posts, moot halls, counting houses, bakeries and butchers' shambles have been noted in historic documents;
- Identify and characterise the activity that took place prior to the establishment of the formal market place;
- Characterise the pre-market place environment and an examination of the market place activities, and sanitation standards. Peterborough's regional market role was to be investigated through the analysis of palaeo-environmental evidence;
- Examine Peterborough's regional market role through analysis of artefacts.

Methodology

The purpose of the investigation was to provide a record of archaeological remains that could not be preserved *in situ* during the proposed development scheme. The investigation required pre-emptive excavation of the fountain array areas and targeted monitoring of construction groundwork by maintaining a watching brief during works in sensitive areas, and recording significant archaeological remains in detail where disturbance was unavoidable.

Works were undertaken with the close cooperation of the contractors, Osborne. The construction excavations and works adhered to basic engineering requirements, but adapted to ground conditions, service locations, etc. encountered at the time of excavation. The approach to archaeological recording responded flexibly to such adaptations and targeted areas and deposits according to their vulnerability to damage and significance to the objectives. Where remains could be successfully preserved *in situ* through adaptations to construction design archaeological work was limited to noting the extent and character of preserved remains and monitored the phase of back-filling and consolidation.

The archaeological contractor liaised closely with the groundwork contractors in order to allocate recording effort efficiently and to avoid disruption to the construction schedule. Any exceptional finds or issues were brought to the attention of the Peterborough City Council Project Supervisor and Site Supervisor. The City Archaeologist was available to assist in field decisions about the necessary level of recording and preservation options.

The work was carried out in accordance to the Institute for Archaeologists' *Code of Conduct* (IfA 2008, 2009 and 2010) and standards for both excavation and watching brief and finds work (IfA 2008a, 2008b, 2008c). Recording followed standard Northamptonshire Archaeology procedures (NA 2006). An Updated Project Design was produced in 2012 to inform the final report (Morris and Yates 2012).

Fountain area excavation

The development included the construction of a fountain array comprising two triangular areas of 15 and 10 fountain risers, respectively. The fountain array is in Cathedral Square immediately east of the Old Guildhall and is fed by pipes from an underground pump room which was built in the disused public toilets north-west of the Old Guildhall (Fig 1.2).

The two triangular areas which encompassed the array of fountain risers, of 140m2 and 115m2, were excavated to 0.75m to 1.2m below ground level and were surrounded by a circuit of pipe trenches 1m to 2m wide and between 0.9m and 1.5m deep. The pipe trenches to feed the risers were excavated to 0.9m deep in corridors 0.70m wide. The fountain array was fed by a pipe trench *c.*20m long by 3m wide and 1.5m to 1.7m deep.

Detailed watching brief

The construction works comprised the removal of the current paving slabs, the diversion of telecommunications cables and other buried utilities, the excavation of drainage channels and gullies, and the deposition of construction materials and new paving. The works took in the whole of Cathedral Square, St John's Square, Church Street, Exchange Street and Cumbergate (Fig 1. 2).

The History and Archaeology of Cathedral Square Peterborough

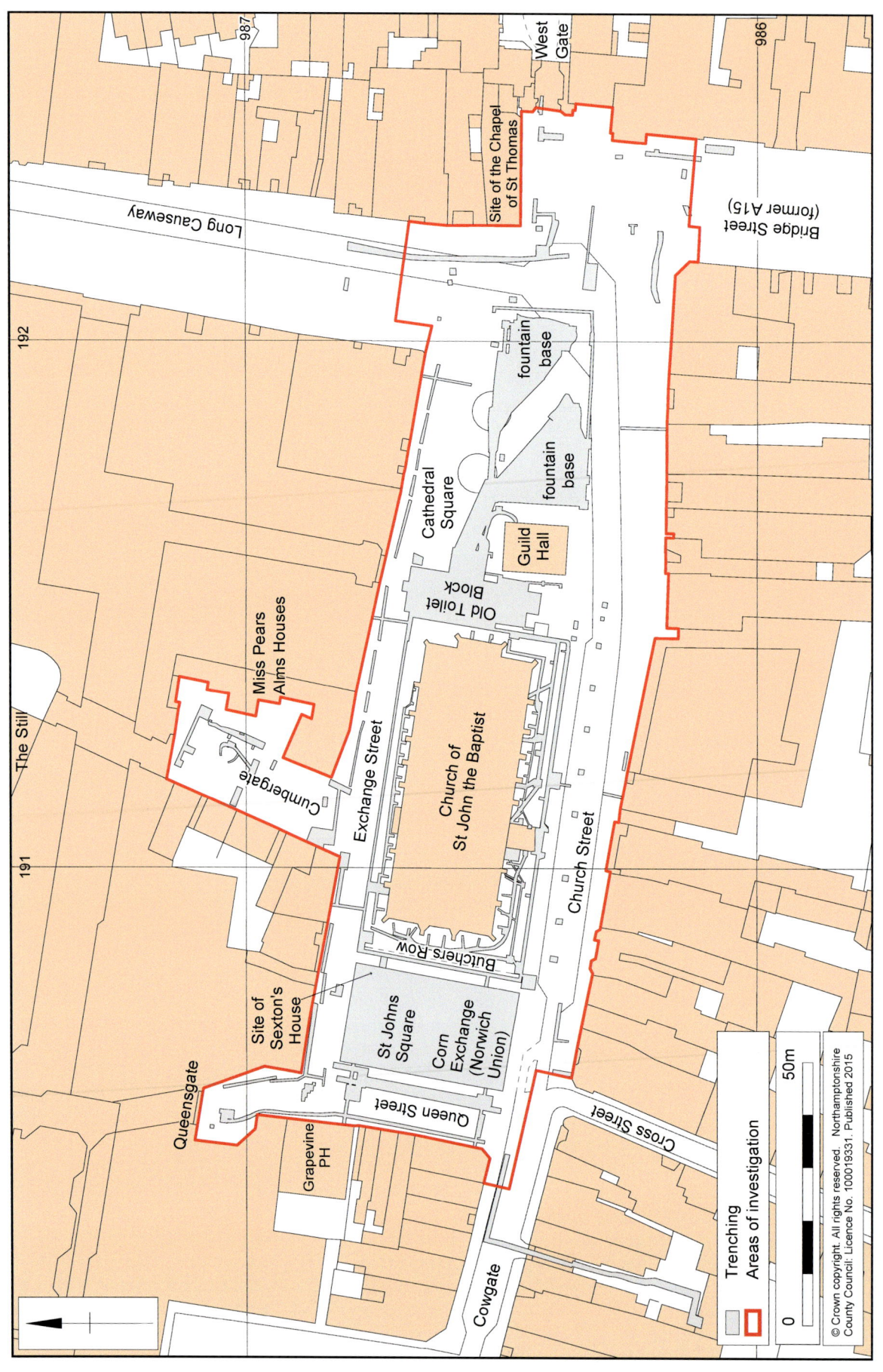

FIG 1.2: DEVELOPMENT AREAS

1. Introduction

The construction excavations extended to about 0.40m below current ground level, but this was modified to lesser depths where necessary and feasible in order to preserve archaeological remains and to avoid disruption to utilities. The diversion and lowering of services and consolidation of soft spots required excavations of varying extents below the general 0.40m construction depth.

The first phase of works involved the excavation of two main drainage channels 0.75m wide, along Church Street and Exchange Street. These were excavated to 1.0m and 2.0m below ground level. They are fed by smaller shallower gullies at 20m intervals. Approximately twenty holes 1.5m square and up to 2m deep were required for inspection chambers. The second element of the scheme was the construction of a pavement circuit 3m wide, around the perimeter of the entire central public realm area and the diversion of shallow services in this area. Deeper service exposure and diversion for the gas main was required at the east end of Cathedral Square, to the west of the Great Gate.

2. Historical background

Prehistory

In the general vicinity of the development area there are several recorded finds comprising two Palaeolithic flints, a Neolithic worked flint, three sets of bronze axes and two Iron Age bronze brooches. A Neolithic stone axe was discovered 200m to the north of the site during trenching in Park Road in 1915. In Chapel Street, 500m north-east of the development area, a shallow pit contained worked flint dating to the middle Bronze Age.

Iron Age and Roman settlement

The major Roman town of *Durobrivae* lies 7km to the east of Peterborough at Water Newton and the Roman fort of Longthorpe lies approximately 3km to the east. A Roman road known as the Fen Causeway linked Water Newton with Denver (near Downham Market). The route of the road is believed to have passed through what is now central Peterborough although its exact course has never been confirmed.

Excavations in City Road, 400m to the north-east of the site, identified a series of ditches, pits and stakeholes of middle Iron Age to Roman date. There is little evidence of Roman activity in Peterborough itself, apart from the remains discovered in City Road, above and another evaluation in City Road that recovered a scatter of Roman pottery, perhaps from manuring of fields.

At the Cathedral, excavations in the 19th and 20th centuries found Romano-British remains including a possible kiln. A watching brief conducted off Wentworth Street, 150m south of the site, recovered some sherds of Roman pottery.

The early monastery

A monastery was established at *Medeshamstead*, (the former name of Peterborough) by King Paeda of Mercia in AD 655 (Mackreth 1994). There is little evidence in the vicinity of the development area for Saxon activity, but a number of Anglo-Saxon settlement and burial sites of the 5th and 6th-centuries have been located south of the Nene between New Fletton and Alwalton.

The early monastery stood on the site occupied by the current cathedral, to the east of the development area. The Anglo-Saxon settlement and market place of *Medeshamstead* lay to the east of the monastery, mainly situated in the Boongate area to the north and east of the abbey precincts. The parish church which served this community was to the east of the abbey precincts.

The Danish raid, the rebuilding of the monastery and the Saxon burh

The original monastery and settlement were sacked in a Danish raid of AD 870, but the rebuilding of the monastic church probably did not begin until after AD 966 under the monastic reforms of Aethelwold, Bishop of Winchester. Excavations at Tout Hill Close, north of the cathedral found a very large pit, possibly used to quarry building stone for the monastery.

Probably between AD 970 and AD 975 earth and timber defences were constructed around the monastery creating a *burh* or walled settlement. These defences appear to have been replaced by a wall at some time during the late 10th or early 11th centuries, as indicated by the Anglo-Saxon Chronicle, which states that Abbot Cenulf (992-1005) put a wall around the monastery for the first time. A stone-built wall foundation, around 2m thick, identified at two points north of the cathedral appeared to have been cut into an earlier revetted bank.

The enclosed *burh* lay approximately 100m to the east of the site. Possible settlement located outside the *burh* defences lay to the north-east at Boongate/Bondgate which included a 'funnel-shaped' market place, although there is some dispute as to the date of foundation (Spoerry and Hinman 1998). After the Norman Conquest the monastery at Peterborough was raided by Hereward in AD 1069.

It is most likely that the *burh* had a west gate which faced inland, away from the fen, as it is thought that Cowgate formed the main route out of the town to the west. This would mean that the development area lay across the route of the thoroughfare and might imply the presence of early medieval settlement within the development area to the west of the monastery. The principal medieval abbey gate, 12th century in date and still in use, faces the new town to the west.

The excavations undertaken at The Still, approximately 100m north of the development area, recorded quarry pits dating to the 11th century (Spoerry and Hinman 1998). A quantity of residual pottery of a similar date was also retrieved suggesting a greater level of activity of this date in the area than the quarry pits alone suggest. The date range of the pottery assemblage recovered from The Still comprises both the post Conquest period and the early to mid-12th century when the main settlement of Peterborough was moved to the western side of the cathedral. The site had evidence of continuous occupation until the present day.

Abbot Martin de Bec and the new monastery

A great fire in Peterborough in AD 1116 destroyed the monastery, *burh* and *vill*. This gave Abbot Martin de Bec the opportunity to rebuild the monastery, extend the monastic boundaries, incorporate the *burh*, and move the town to the west of the monastery. The surrounding medieval streets formed by Hithegate (Bridge Street), Long Causeway, Priestgate, Cowgate, Cumbergate, and Westgate, all date approximately to this time. The boundaries of Westgate and Cowgate are curved, showing where they were taken in from the surrounding fields together with the market square (Fig 1, 1). The market area, the *Marketstede*, was laid out by around 1145 as the focus of de Bec's medieval 'new town' plan. Records suggest the trades and industries that became located in and around the market square included the butchers market at the west end, with by-products producing a skin market, and woolcombers established in the area of Cumbergate/Westgate to the north of the market. Spin-off industries from the skin and wool products included the leather trade, spinning and knitting. A fish market was located on the south side of the square. The development site falls within this historic centre of the city and covers most of the ancient rectangular market area, the eastern part of which is now known as Cathedral Square.

Norman Gate, at the east end of the market place, is situated on the west side of the Cathedral precinct and opens onto Cathedral Square (Fig 2.1). The Norman gateway was constructed between 1177 and 1194, during the time of Abbot Benedict. It was remodelled in the 14th century with the addition of the pointed Gothic arch built in front of the semicircular Norman arch and the flanking turrets. The new arch enabled a portcullis to be incorporated, the slot for which can still be seen.

The Swans Pool, some distance to the north, was split in the new arrangements at the northern edge of the abbey precincts with one channel flowing through the abbey precincts where it would have flushed the monastic toilets before going into the River Nene. The other channel ran along the outside of the western boundary edge of the precincts and formed the 'town ditch' an open sewer which drained south to the river. A bridge crossing an infilled watercourse was exposed to the west of the Great Gate during excavation works to widen Narrow Bridge Street in 1885 and a related feature was exposed again during excavation works for drainage in 1937. The ancient bridge was constructed of Barnack ashlar stone with an arch of *c*.6m, and the observed decoration dated it to the 13th or 14th centuries. The finds recovered from the ditch fill dated from the 14th to mid-17th centuries, when the ditch was filled in.

The church of St John the Baptist

The construction of church of St John the Baptist in the market place was undertaken in the early 15th century to replace the former parish church located to the east of the monastery, which was no longer at the centre of activity in Peterborough (Fig 2.2). This resulted in the demolition of the 'old' parish church and the Chapel of St Thomas the Martyr (Thomas Becket) to provide material for the construction of the new parish church. The site of St John's was a prominent one in the Marketstead, the place traditionally thought to be occupied by butchers' stalls, where the ground was considered too contaminated by butchery waste and blood. The depression in which the church sits was possibly dug out to cleanse the site, and at least partly a result of later ground build-up in the

FIG 2.1: THE NORMAN OR WEST GATE TO THE CATHEDRAL PRECINCT IN 2009, PRIOR TO DEVELOPMENT, LOOKING EAST

Fig 2.2: The Church of St John the Baptist and the Guildhall in 2009, Prior to development, looking south-west

surrounding market and streets, or perhaps to ensure that the altar was on a lower level than the abbey church. The parish cemetery was thought to have been established in the abbey precincts to the north of the abbey church, later the cathedral.

The findings from excavations on the north side of Exchange Street have been taken to support the proposition that the church sits in a purpose-made depression, as there was no demonstrable build-up of material that could be dated to the medieval period. Excavations within the vicinity of the site, such as those at The Still (Spoerry and Hinman 1998) and the Queensgate Centre and Westgate Arcade (Casa-Hatton *et al* 2007), all within 120m of the study site, have revealed up to 1.6m of stratigraphy dating from the late medieval period to the present day.

Observations of a service trench excavated through the eastern end of Cathedral Square in 2007 revealed made ground to a depth exceeding 1.0m (B Robinson pers comm). The upper 0.5m of these deposits was demonstrably modern, but no dating evidence was recovered for the lower layers which may represent former surfaces to the Marketstead. A short length of stone wall foundation was also seen in this service trench 1.0m below current ground level.

The dissolution of the monastery

Peterborough monastery was closed in 1539 as part of the Reformation. In 1541 the monastery church became a Cathedral of the new diocese of Peterborough. Prior to the reformation the administration of the market, the upkeep and the good repair of the public buildings, highways and bridges was the responsibility of the Abbot of the monastery, but in the early 1570s this became the charge of a newly established local secular governing body known as the Feoffees. The function of the Feoffees were to raise funding to pay taxes of the 40 poorest residents, repair and maintain the church, to repair roads and buildings and to fund charitable bodies that benefit the town.

John Speed's map of 1610

The earliest known map of the city, produced by John Speed in 1610, gives a good impression of the extent and character of the later medieval town (Fig 2.3). The layout of the market place at this time is assumed to have remained relatively unchanged. It has the characteristic narrow medieval burgage plots which define the perimeter of the market place and the frontages of the neighbouring streets which are obvious features of 19th-century maps of the city centre. A covered Butter Cross or Butter Market (butter, eggs and poultry) is depicted in Cathedral Square, one of the three buildings depicted in the market place to the east of the church. The Butter Cross was a covered area to be rented out by traders, to the east of St John's, probably in the location of the present Guildhall. In 1572 the Butter Cross was run by the Feoffees. The structure between the Butter Cross and St John's Church would appear to be a market cross. A market cross is mentioned in town books of 1614 and 1649 but had apparently disappeared by 1699, probably with the building of the Guildhall in 1671 (Fig 2.4). The function of the remaining building in the south-east corner of the market place is not known. Speed's plan also shows a line of buildings to the immediate west of the church in an area later known as Butchers Row.

The Feoffees were also responsible for two other buildings that were also leased out, a moot hall which stood where Miss Pears' Alms Houses (Figs 2.6, 2.7 and 3.38) now stand on the edge of the market and Cumbergate (Mackreth 1994) and an earlier guildhall than the currently named structure, the location of which is unknown. In celebration of the restoration of Charles II, a subscription was raised for a public cross or town house which resulted in the building of the present Guildhall in the market place on the site of the earlier Butter Cross, to the east side of the church. It was built by John Lovin in 1670-1 and was originally known as the Chamber over the Cross. In 1874 it became the first town hall, with the council changing its name to the Guildhall in 1876.

Thomas Eyre's map of 1721

Thomas Eyre's map of Peterborough, published in 1721, provides a comparatively detailed survey of the town at that time (Fig 2.5). The structures shown on Speed's map in the square, to the east of the church, are gone. The

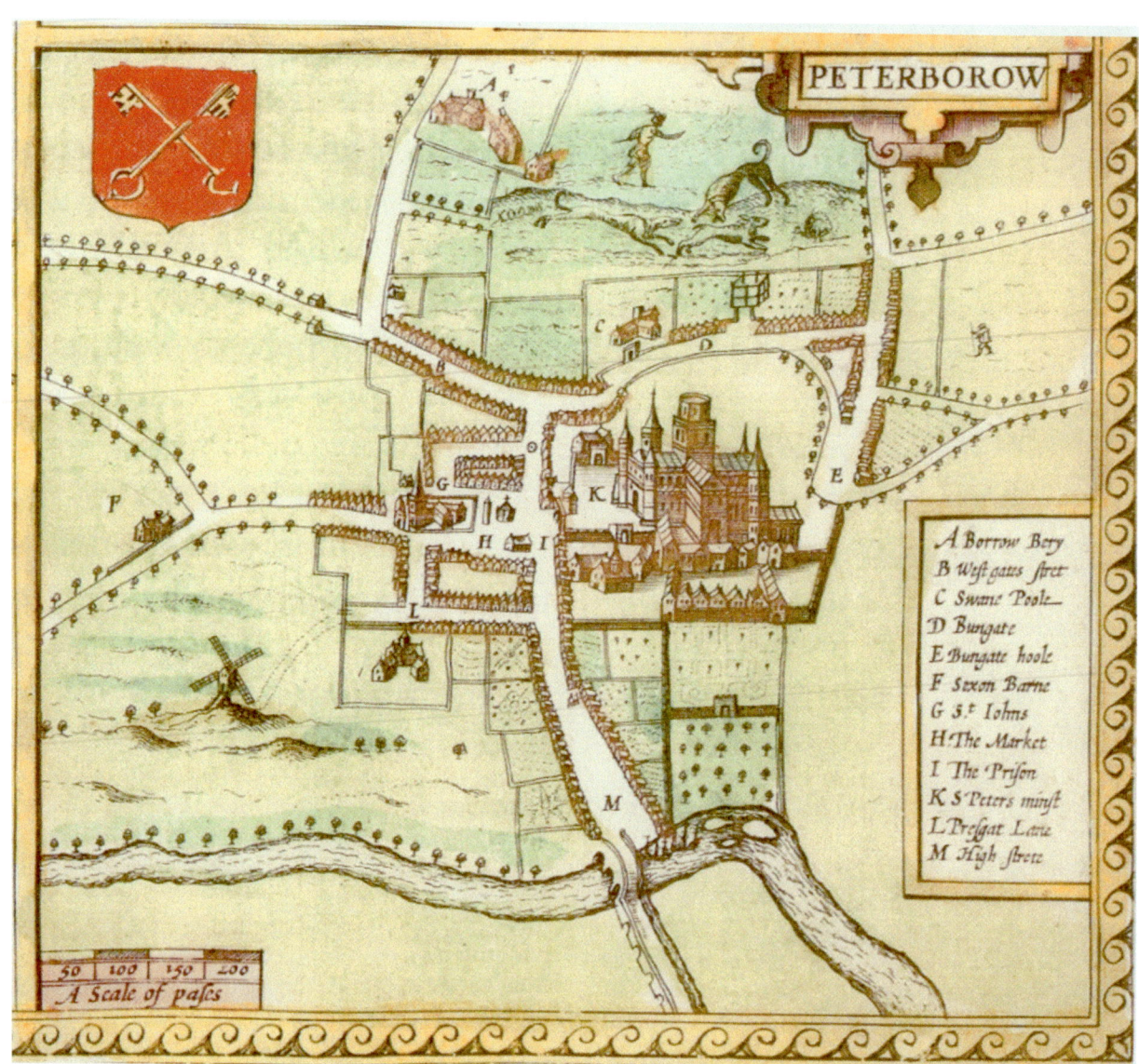

Fig 2.3: John Speed's Map of Peterborough, 1610 (Peterborough Museum)

Fig 2.4: The Guildhall, built in 1671, looking south-west

Guildhall is shown with a row of buildings between it and St John's Church. To the west of the church, there is Butchers Row or 'shambles', with the Sexton's house extending into the churchyard at the north end. To the west of Butchers Row the map shows a new block of buildings separated from Butchers Row by a narrow lane and alleyway.

By the end of the 18th century, the streets were in a poor state from the lack of clearance and repair. In 1789 the Feoffees, the body accountable for the maintenance of the roads, paid 500 pounds to be relieved of their responsibilities, which were taken over by the Peterborough Pavement and Improvement Commission that was established in 1790. Their first act included the right to enforce the streets to be cleared of signs that caused a hindrance, to compulsory purchase and demolish buildings and the creation of footpaths for pedestrians. At the first meeting the commission announced their surveyor, Francis Carter of London, for the resurfacing of the streets and advertisements were made asking for cobbles, Yorkshire flagstones and kerbstones. The cobbles, which were known as 'petrified kidneys', were rammed into gravel to form a surface, while the flagstones were used for the footpaths consisting of two stones 4 feet wide with 3 inch kerbs (1.22m wide with 77mm kerbs) (Tebbs 1997).

The result of these new market and street surfaces was the creation of a much improved atmosphere throughout the city centre, making it a pleasant and easier place to access and pass through. This was remarked upon by Celia Fiennes a renowned lady traveller and writer of that time, when passing through Peterborough in 1798,

> '...the streets are clean and neat, well-pitched and broad as one will see anywhere. There is a very spacious market place, a good Cross and Town Hall'.

The Peterborough Enclosure Map of 1821 (not illustrated) shows the site including the Guildhall and the row of buildings between the Guildhall and the Church of St John the Baptist. The block of buildings to the west of Butchers Row had become dominated by a single building, presumably the theatre, which stood on the site from 1798-99 to 1846 when it was bought by the promoters of the Corn Exchange.

The Municipal Borough Council, 1874

A major political change came to Peterborough in 1874, with the Act of Incorporation creating a Municipal Borough Council and its first mayor, Henry Pearson Gates. This new local government was a response to the rapidly developing and expanding

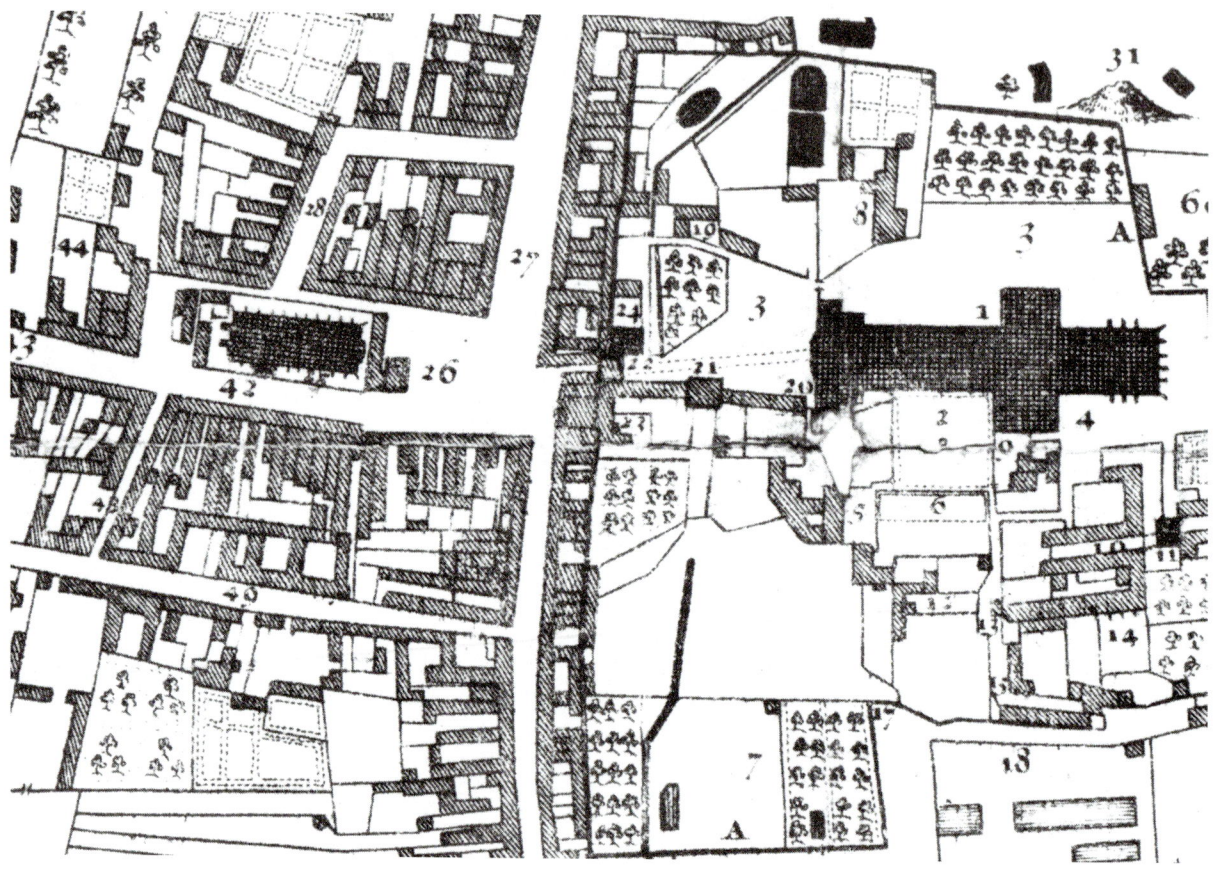

Fig 2.5: Thomas Eyre's Map of Peterborough, 1721

Fig 2.6: Miss Frances Pears' Almshouses (now Harriet's Tearooms) on Exchange Street, looking north-east

1. Introduction

Fig 2.7: The plaque dedicated by the Foeffees to Miss Frances Pears for her funding to assist the aged and infirm of the parish of Peterborough

Fig 2.8: The Gates Memorial, moved from Cathedral Square to Bishops Road Gardens in 1963, looking north

city, especially after the railways arrived in the 1840s, which brought about the growth of industry and caused the population to greatly increase. With this growth, the requirement for the water supplies increased along with a greater demand for gas and electricity for lighting and power, which required new subterranean pipe and cable services. The disposal of sewerage and surface water also required the construction of buried drains and culverts.

The theatre was demolished and replaced with the new Corn Exchange building which opened on 30 September 1846. Over the following years the building increased in size, firstly to the north in 1855 and later extended to the east in 1870. Finally the north-east corner was completed in 1893, removing the final remnant of Butchers Row and the Sexton's House. An alleyway was created between the Corn Exchange and the churchyard wall. The Corn Exchange was known to have extensive cellars

Fig 2.9: Peterborough City Hall, built in the 1930s on the newly created Bridge Street, looking east

Fig 2.10: Cathedral Square, looking east, from the tower of the Church of St John the Baptist in 1919 (the Francis Frith collection)

Fig 2.11: Cathedral Square, looking east, from the tower of the Church of St John the Baptist in 2009

that were rented out to brewers and wine merchants in order to generate income. The present Cathedral Square, east of the Guildhall, remained the city's main market place and was largely free of major structures until the construction of an elaborate lamp-post, which was replaced by the Gates Memorial in 1897 (Fig 2.8). The memorial was a fountain, honouring the city's first mayor, Henry Pearson Gates.

The twentieth century

In 1964 the Corn Exchange was demolished, with the Norwich Union building taking its place in 1966. The Gates Memorial of 1897 remained a market place landmark until it was removed to Bishop's Road gardens in 1963, when the weekly market was moved to the old cattle market.

During the 1930s the east side of Narrow Street/Narrow Bridge Street was removed creating a broad open thoroughfare thereafter known as Bridge Street. The new City Hall was also located on the eastern side of this road (Fig 2.9). The development involved the clearance of buildings on the eastern side of the site, extending up to the Cathedral Gate (Figs 2.10 and 2.11). The post war period also saw the demolition of the buildings behind the Guildhall. The main A15/47 road routes passed through the city centre (Long Causeway, Church Street, Cowgate and Bridge Street) until the late 20th century, when they were diverted from the centre of Peterborough.

It was during the early 1960s that a new fountain was constructed, as shown on the 1967 Ordnance Survey map, which also shows underground toilets and an electricity substation to the east of St John's Church in the area formerly occupied by buildings of the 18th century. The development of the Queensgate Shopping Centre in the late 1970s supplanted a large part of the street plan and commercial district on the north side of Cathedral Square and Cowgate across to Westgate, the Queensgate Centre opened in 1982. More recently, the fountain in Cathedral Square was replaced by a pair of circular raised flower beds (Figs 2.2 and 2.4).

3. The Archaeology of Cathedral Square

The archaeological evidence from the numerous individual excavations and watching brief interventions is brought together to provide a narrative describing the development of Cathedral Square. The detailed archaeological record that lies behind this overview appears as a series of in-depth narratives that are available as appendices to the client report (Morris 2016), which is available online through the Archaeology Data Service (ADS).

Archaeological interventions and summary chronology

The archaeological work identified a series of extensive stone surfaces, beginning with the creation of the market square and the 'new town' in the 12th century by Abbot de Bec and continuing through to the 19th century. See Table 3.1, page 48, for a concise tabulation of the known historical developments and the recorded archaeology.

The medieval cobble surface of the market square became overlaid by an accumulation of extensive fine black silty organic deposit, containing pottery dated to the 16th century.

At the start of the 15th century the parish church of St John the Baptist had been constructed at the west end of the medieval market square with a cemetery to the west between the church and Queensgate. Seven burials were found, but much of the cemetery had been lost to later activity. The churchyard was enclosed by a stone wall, the remains of which were identified to the south and west of the church. Adjacent to the south side of the church, the medieval Church Street comprised a roughly metalled road and path separated by a kerb of large stone slabs.

To the south of the market square were the remains of a stone-walled building dating from the late 15th to 17th centuries. It contained well preserved beaten floors of clay and mortar, with the suggestion of internal partitions. Window glass and wall plaster was recovered from the floors. Adjacent to this building in Cathedral Square were pitched-stone path surfaces. To the west of the church a small area of internal floor surfaces were the probable remains of a building that formed part of Butchers Row.

The late 17th century saw the construction of the Guildhall to the east of the church. A trench adjacent to the east side of the Guildhall, revealed a length of curving stone foundation. Associated with the Guildhall was the raising of the ground level and resurfacing of the square with compacted limestone fragments. This also resulted in the removal of the previous building tenements on the south side of the square. In the late 18th or early 19th centuries the square was again raised and resurfaced.

This surface was constructed of pitched limestone, with shallow gullies to facilitate drainage. A surface of granite setts from the 19th century lay below the slab pavement of the 20th century.

Anglo-Saxon activity (7th to 11th centuries)

The underlying natural geology

The presence of the underlying limestone meant construction material was readily available in the vicinity of the site, and quarry pits have been identified in previous excavations. At The Still (Spoerry & Hinman 1998) there was a series of quarry pits dating from the 11th century and excavations at Tout Hill Close found a large quarry pit, possibly for stone for the building of the monastery. The natural clay and river terrace sands and gravels that overlie the limestone were encountered throughout the excavations.

A lack of buried soil

In the few places where the natural geology was exposed, there was an absence of overlying soils in all the archaeological areas, encompassing the market square and parts of the contemporary street plan.

The natural drift deposits were either overlaid directly by the introduced stone market/street surfaces of Abbot de Bec's 'new town' or were cut by contemporary features. The lack of buried soil would seem to suggest that there had been large scale stripping down to the natural clay or the sand and gravels. In places the gravels were re-deposited over the exposed clay to form a more stable sub-base for the market/street surfacing.

The one exception for the presence of a buried soil was a potential layer over natural clay in an alleyway on the south side of Cowgate, an area probably beyond the 'new towns' initial expansion to the west, but no dating material was recovered from the deposit.

Early features

Two features, a wooden post (not retrieved) in its posthole, at the east end of Cathedral Square (Figs 3.1 and 3.2) and a large pit to the west of the church of St John the Baptist, were both sealed below the market square stone surfaces that probably dates to De Bec's 'New Town'.

Though only two pre-market features were identified, this does not necessarily indicate that the land to the west of the Anglo-Saxon *burh* was not being used or occupied in the pre-Conquest period, but that the soil horizons that could have contained evidence of settlement had

Fig 3.1: Posthole with *in situ* wooden post, at the east end of Cathedral Square

been later stripped off. Also, the limited exposure of pre-market square levels during the development much reduced the opportunity of identifying Anglo-Saxon or earlier activity in this area.

Abbot Martin de Bec's 'New Town' (12th-14th centuries)

The New Town

The development of Abbot de Bec's new town was the first major event in the growth and expansion of Peterborough since the establishment of the monastery and *burh*.

The creation of the planned town, after the fire of 1116, occurred in *c.*1145, when a large rectangular open market square (marketsteade) was established immediately to the west of the *burh*, centred on the Cathedral Gateway. The market square was 200m (1 furlong) long and *c.*50m wide, and therefore two acres in extent, with a grid plan of streets laid out around the square. The footprint of the modern development included all of this area and Cumbergate, a part of the 'new town' street plan. The creation of the market place and new grid plan of streets was just one of many planned towns being created throughout the country in the 12th century, which was a flourishing period in the history of the English towns (Poole 1951).

Abbot de Bec's market square, 1145

The early market square appears to have more or less retained its shape, but was then inclusive of the area later to be occupied by the Parish Church of St John the Baptist at the western end of the square, Church Street and Exchange Street to the south and north sides of the church respectively, along with St John's Square and Queen Street. The east part of the market square still forms an open area now known as Cathedral Square, in which the Guildhall stands on the west side, close to the church.

The early market place and streets were identified as remnant surfaces of stone cobbles occurring throughout the development area directly overlying the natural clay or gravel (Fig 3.3). Some natural gravel was deposited over the exposed clay to form a stable make-up layer or sub-base to the stone surface, though it is possible the gravel may have formed an initial surface in its own right. The surface was largely composed of cobbles of worn, sub-angular to rounded limestone chips and fragments and occasional blocks, 0.05-0.25m, rounded cobbles/pebbles, 0.01-0.10m, and gravel, with variations in its composition across the market place. The thickness of the surface was between 0.05m and 0.20m and in places it had been heavily worn, exposing the underlying natural. The surface was firm to very compact, slightly uneven, but it was generally level, though it had a perceptible incline following the natural slope to the south and east.

Although the surface dates from the mid-12th century, the pottery retrieved from some areas is dated as late as the 17th century, suggesting a constant process of maintenance and repair throughout this period. Other material found compressed into this surface included animal bone, wood and brick/tile fragments (Fig 3.3). Shallow slots in the surface were probably wheel ruts, aligned approximately east-west, suggesting a well-used track across the square.

The Cumbergate street surface to the north, which had a similar composition to the market square make-up, displayed a slight rise towards the eastern street frontage, but it was otherwise fairly level, opening onto the north side of the market square.

The Norman or West Gate of the Cathedral precinct

The Norman or West Gate is situated on the west side of the Cathedral precincts. The gateway, which is Romanesque in style, was constructed between 1177 and 1194 during the time of Abbot Benedict. It has a semi-circular rib vault of one bay, with moulded semi-circular arches on the east and west, and wall arcades inside on the north and south. A doorway in the south wall of the gateway leads to steps up to the chapel of St Nicholas, which occupies the room above.

The gateway was remodelled by Abbot Godfrey de Crowland (1299-1322) in the 14th century with the addition of the pointed Gothic arch built in front of the semi-circular Norman arch and the flanking turrets at the angles which were broadened or added. Above the gate arch is a wall arcade with cinquefoil arches. The new west wall enabled a portcullis to be incorporated, the slot for which can still be seen. It was also due to Abbot

3. The Archaeology of Cathedral Square

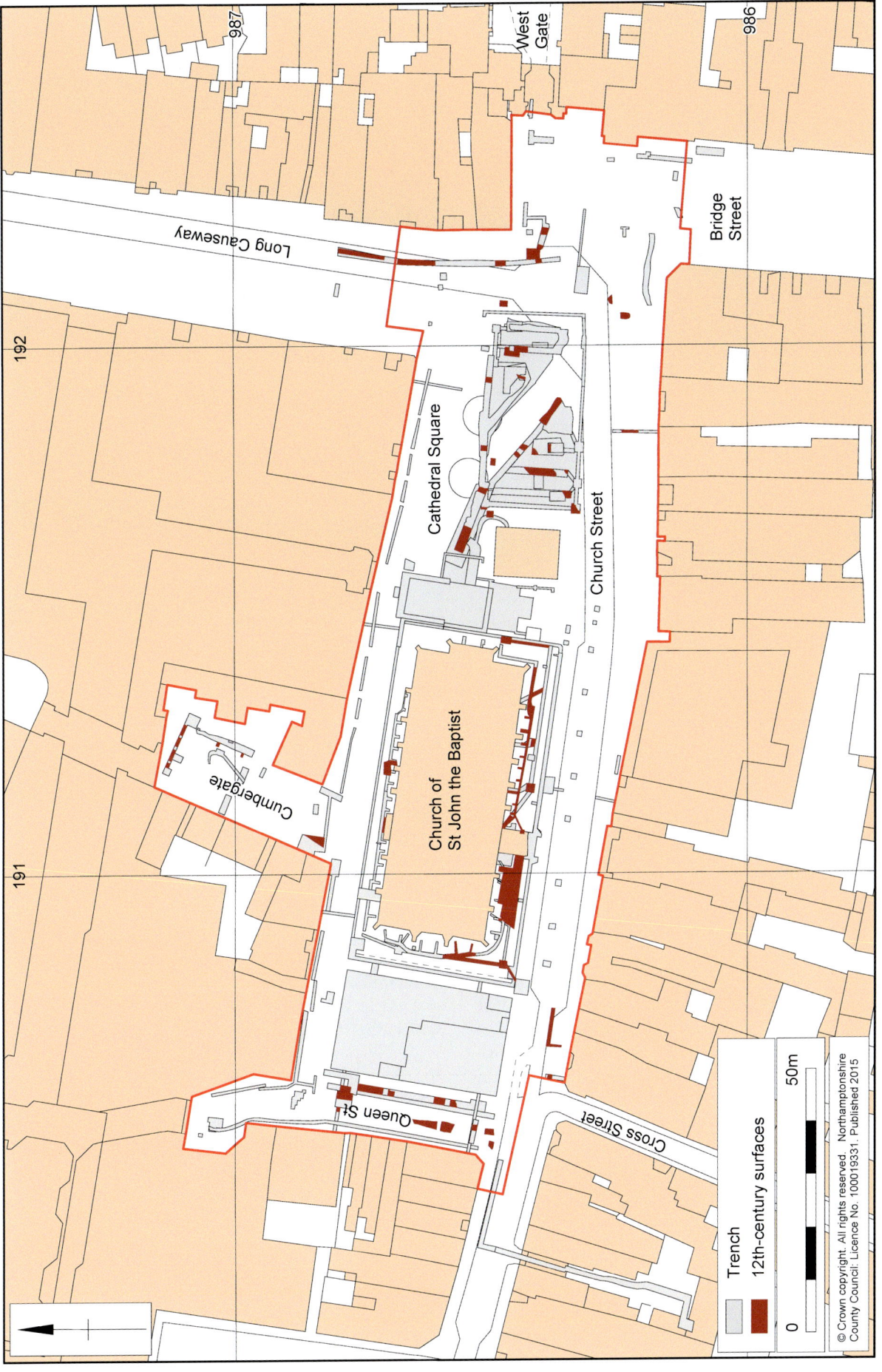

Fig 3.2: Survival of the 12th-century Market Square surface

Fig 3.3: de Bec's Market Square surface, sealed by dark silt of the 12th to 17th centuries, Cathedral Square, looking west

Fig 3.4: Gas trench at the cathedral west gate, showing stone foundations of the 12th to 14th centuries, looking north-east

Godfrey de Crowland who, in 1307, allowed for the first time permanent housing and shops to be built along the east side of Hithegate (Bridge Street), against the precinct wall and the wall around his private garden, that backed on to the street, which previously, may have only had temporary structures and stalls (Mackreth 1994).

The construction of the gateway appears to postdate the creation of the 'new town' and the market square by over 30 years, but it would seem unlikely that there was not an existing entrance at this site, leading into the market square.

The stone foundations from the 12th and 14th centuries were exposed during reopening of the gas main trench that passed through the gateway into the Cathedral precincts (Fig 3.4). The foundations for the supporting 14th-century south turret were exposed during groundwork in 1.0m-deep trenches along the street frontage to the west (Fig 3.5). The foundations for the north turret had been partly replaced with concrete, probably in the 1930s, during widening and construction of new Bridge Street.

The impact of the gateway was diminished in later centuries, as the eastern frontages of Bridge Street and the Long Causeway to the south and north were relocated further westward, impinging on the original broad street, leaving only a narrow lane for access. The gateway was not given greater visual exposure again until the widening of new Bridge Street in the 1930s.

The watercourse and the Cathedral Gateway Bridge

The path of the 'town-ditch' had lain outside the Norman Gate, draining southwards to the river, until it was backfilled in the 17th century. Records indicate that a bridge was built over the ditch between the market place and the gateway during the 13th or 14th centuries. Neither this watercourse nor the bridge were seen during development, but several large blocks of disturbed ashlar stone observed in the side of the gas main trench close to the Cathedral Gateway would have been close to the location of the bridge. The stone was probably placed here during 19th or 20th-century building works.

The Chapel of St Thomas the Martyr

The present building on the north side of the Gateway, originally built as a bank, is on the site of the nave of the Chapel of St Thomas the Martyr (Thomas Becket). The construction of the chapel was started by the Abbot of Peterborough, William de Waterville (1155-1175), shortly after the martyrdom of the archbishop in 1170. The chapel was completed under Abbot Benedict (1177-1194), who was at Canterbury when Thomas Becket was murdered and brought a number of relics of the archbishop to Peterborough. These were placed in the chancel of the 'new' chapel. The chapel spanned the western wall of the

3. The Archaeology of Cathedral Square

Fig 3.5: Foundation of the south turret of the 14th-century West Gate, partially disturbed by services of the early 20th century, looking south-east

ancient *burh*, on the north side of the Gateway, with the nave extending westwards into De Bec's Market Place (Marketsteade). It can only be concluded that the nave crossed the course of the town ditch, which must have been contained in a culvert beneath the building.

Two lengths of wall/foundations aligned east-west with a surface between them were exposed in a trench close to the eastern building frontages on Long Causeway (Fig 3.6). Both were in poor condition, partly damaged by the existing gas main trench and abutted by backfill material. It is possible that these walls were related to the chapel, perhaps a covered porch at the west end of the nave.

The chapel became very popular as a place of worship with the townspeople, with the more distant and sometimes difficult to access parish church to the east of the *burh*, losing out in number of parishioners due to poor roads and flooding and in turn the amount of donations declined.

This resulted in a dispute between the parish vicar and the chapel establishment, which was not resolved until the early 15th century, when the nave of the chapel that lay on the market square side of the gateway and the old parish church were both demolished to provide material for the construction of the new Parish Church of St John the Baptist on the western half of the market place.

The construction of the new parish church divided the market place into exact halves. The distance from the east wall of the churchyard to the west side of Queen Street and east to the entrance of the Great Gate, was 97.5m each way. The reduction of the market place to half its size was significant, in that it probably meant that either the markets were forced into a smaller area or that all the space was no longer required for the market, with perhaps many of the stall holders and stands having become established as shops in the burgage plots around the market place and the church.

Medieval features along Cumbergate

The only other feature apparently contemporary with the early development phase was the stone front wall of a property on the east side of Cumbergate and a nearby pit, which contained Lyvden/Stanion pottery of the 12th to 13th centuries. However, the wall was undated and could belong to a later phase of activity (Fig 3.7). This early frontage was to survive into the 20th century when it was defined by brick wall 1577.

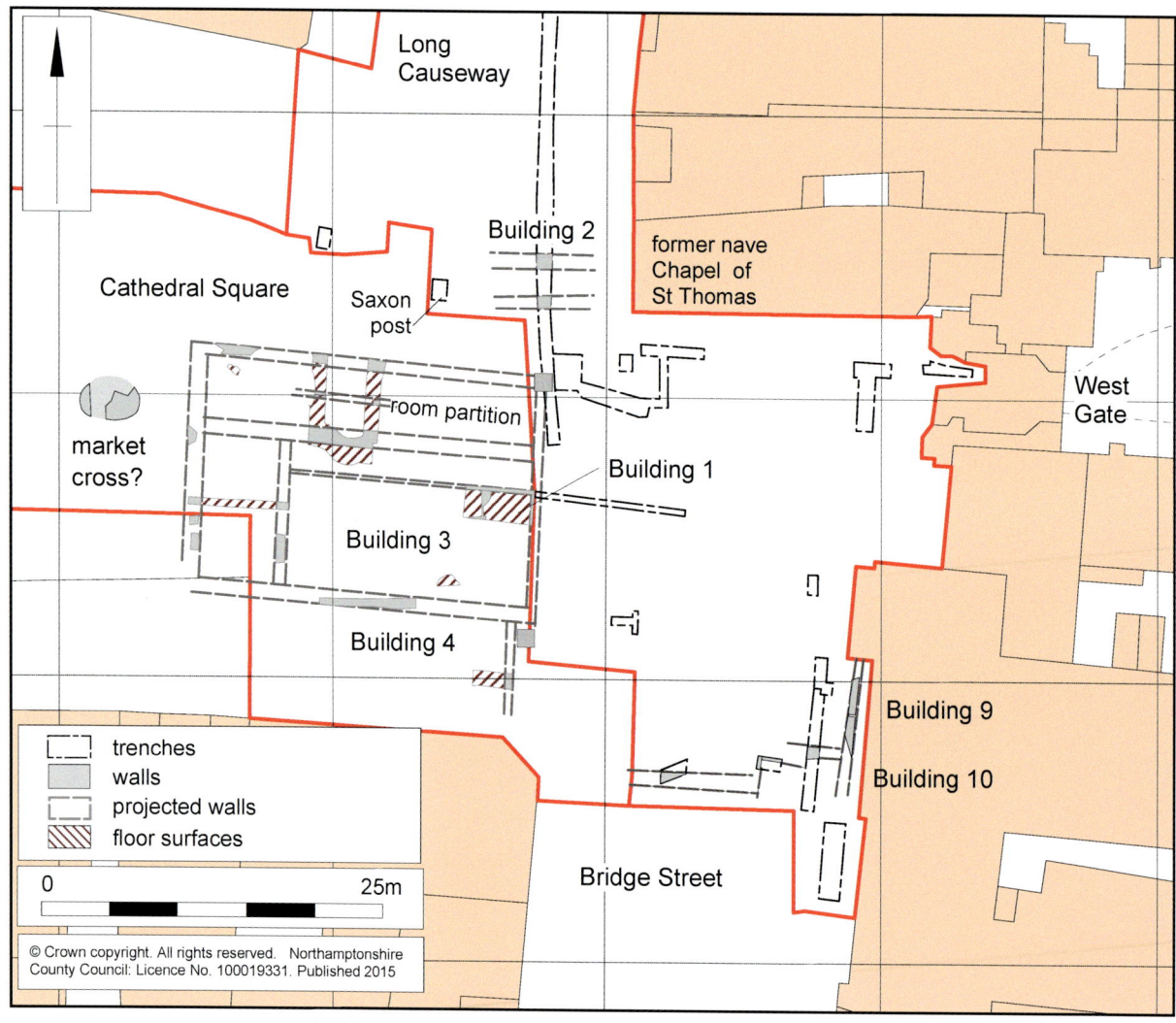

Fig 3.6: Buildings at the east end of Cathedral Square

A medieval building (Building 1)

On the south side of Cathedral Square the remains of a stone wall, aligned north-south, was flanked by what appeared to be the early market square surface, making it contemporary with the early square or possibly even pre-dating it (Fig 3.6). The wall was set on a stone foundation offset from the wall, within a construction trench, suggesting it was part of a substantial structure. A rough stone packing over the robbed wall contained fragments of a millstone, perhaps forming part of the foundations for Building 3. Abutting the west side of the wall were three surfaces, the upper of which was a rough stone external surface which tipped gently southwards and westwards away from the wall face, possibly the market square. No dating evidence was recovered from these layers, but they were sealed by a silt deposit containing pottery dated from the 13th-15th centuries.

Dark organic street silts

The market square probably formed the secular and commercial centre of the 'new town', with weekly markets and narrow burgage plots surrounding the square. The waste from the tenements and the market, especially from the animal market, appears to have been dumped within the market square with a lack of will or resources, from initially the church and later the secular governing bodies, to keep the streets clear of debris.

The result of this accumulation was the formation of an extensive fine black silty organic deposit spread across the square, largely sealing the stone market square surface (Figs 3.8 and 3.9). The deposit included the occasional small stone and gravel, household waste and animal dung and formed a substantial layer, 0.1m to 0.4m deep, making the stone surface generally redundant. The deposit as excavated still had a pungent odour, and when wet it became soft and sticky, and the streets of central Peterborough would have been reduced to a stinking bog. Arbitrary attempts to partially resurface the square using spreads of stone over the dark deposit appear to have been ineffective as they became enveloped by more silt in the growing accumulation.

3. THE ARCHAEOLOGY OF CATHEDRAL SQUARE

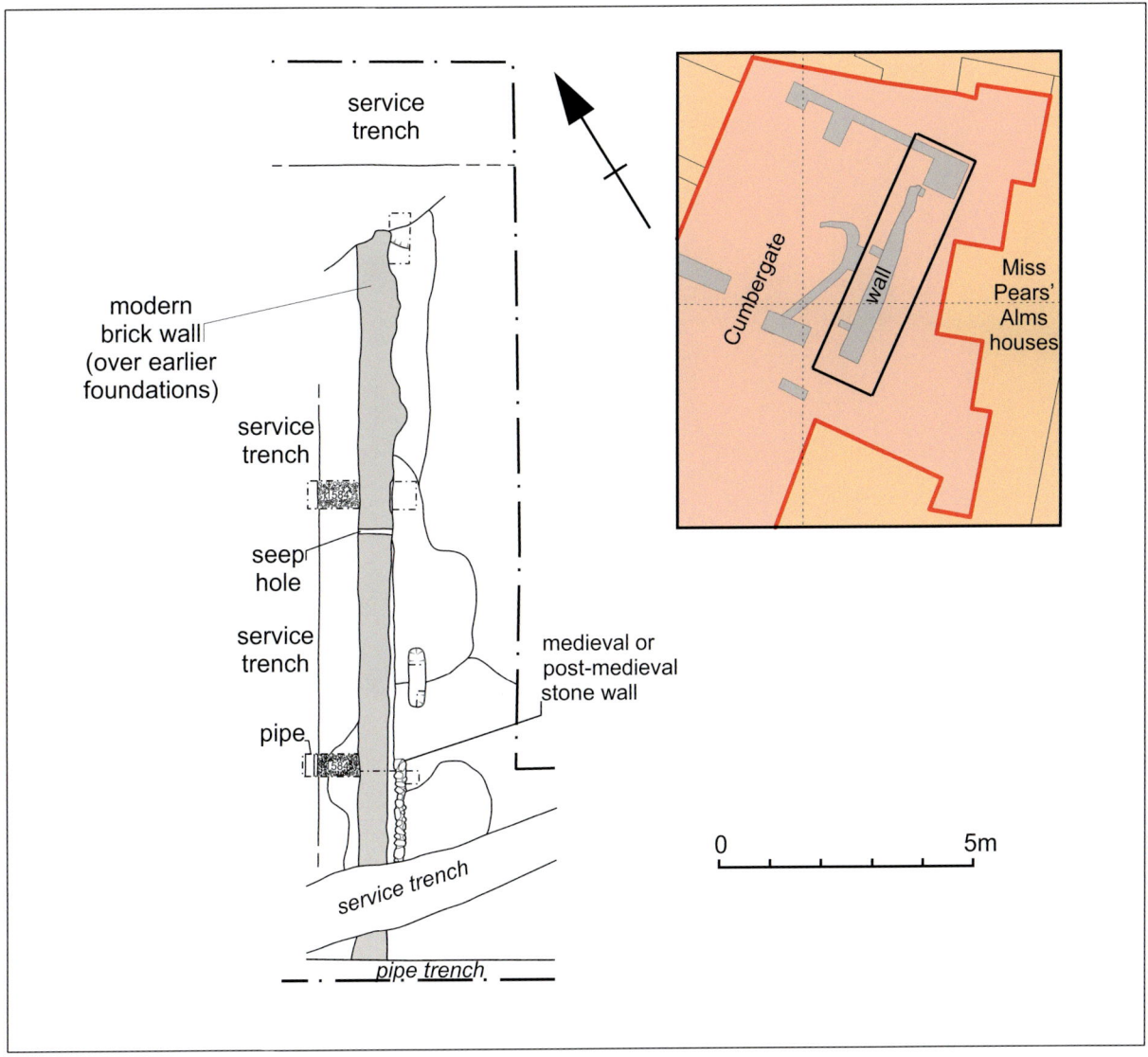

FIG 3.7: MEDIEVAL AND POST-MEDIEVAL STREET FRONTAGES ALONG CUMBERGATE

The pottery recovered from the deposit dates from the 12th-17th centuries, but was predominately Bourne D ware (1450-1637), indicating that the final period of accumulation was through the 16th century. The deposit also contained a variety of other finds comprising animal bone, brick, tile, household artefacts and street losses, which included a copper alloy purse bar of Tudor date, a 15th-century thimble, an iron key, a candle holder, a riding spur, a buckle, numerous nails and a quantity of worked leather fragments, including shoe remains (see Fig 4.6), with an assemblage of late medieval turn-shoe parts and waste leather in the dark silt layer on the edge of the market square and Long Causeway to the east (see Fig 4.7).

The church of St John the Baptist (15th century)

The new parish church

Construction of the new parish church at the west end of the medieval market square, was undertaken during the early years of the 15th century (1402-1407), moving the parish church to the heart of the then well-established town of Peterborough, although the church's location meant the reduction of the market square to half its original size.

Anecdotal evidence says the area of the church site was cleared of the blood contaminated ground (dark silt) left by the butchers' market, leaving an excavated hollow in which the church was constructed. The contaminated material may have been disposed of by dumping and levelling it on land adjacent to the south side of Cumbergate, where a layer of material 0.5m to 0.6m deep was seen during excavations in 2001 (Casa Hatton *et al* 2007), similar to the market square silt deposit and also over an early street/yard surface.

Even if the area of the church and churchyard was partly dug out to remove contaminated ground, this would not explain why the Church level today is so much lower

FIG 3.8: DARK SILT OVER DE BEC'S MARKET SQUARE SURFACE, ON THE NORTH SIDE OF CATHEDRAL SQUARE

FIG 3.9: DE BEC'S MARKET SQUARE SURFACE, WITH OVERLYING DARK SILT AND SHOWING LATER RESURFACING

than the surrounding streets. Excavation on Church Street has shown that in the 15th century the churchyard and street levels were comparable and it was the subsequent accumulation of silts and resurfacing through to the 18th century that raised the ground levels around the southern half of the churchyard (see Fig 3.15).

The excavations around the church showed that the market square was far from level. Within the trenching at the east end of the churchyard, de Bec's market square surface was seen about 1.0m below the ground and church floor level, at 6.90m aOD, so the church foundation had to be raised above the market square level. The surface at the west end of the churchyard was 0.40m below the church floor level at 7.50m aOD, and continuing to rise, displaying an incline from the market square to the east, draining towards the town ditch.

To the south and west of the church the remains of a contemporary stone churchyard wall was evident, lying parallel to and about 6.0m away from the church façade (Figs 3.10 and 3.11). No evidence of an early corresponding wall was observed on the north and east sides of the church. Slightly green organic rich soils appear to have been introduced to level up the ground around the church. On the surface of the lower soil layer there was a thin spread of gravel, which may have been an early churchyard surface. Pottery recovered from these layers dates from the 15th-16th centuries. Similar soil layers were not present on the north side of the church.

A previously unknown cemetery

To the west of the churchyard wall a remnant of cemetery had been preserved beneath a later path in an area measuring 10m north-south by 2.3m east-west, lying between later drainage trenches. There were an estimated 17 graves, all aligned east-west (Fig 3.11). This is likely to be a small remnant of a once larger cemetery. Seven burials had human bone visible, and pottery from the grave fills dated from the 13th to 18th centuries was recovered (Figs 3.10 and 3.11). Some of the pottery was likely to be residual, while the later sherds were likely to be intrusive.

The ground to the west of this had been heavily truncated by building development from the 19th-century, and more recently, removing the western extent of the cemetery. However, the level of the cemetery appeared to have been built up in a similar fashion to the churchyard with the introduction of cess-stained

Fig 3.10: Early churchyard wall, north side of Church Street, looking north

green soils through which the graves were subsequently cut. Records suggest that the church of St John the Baptist never had a burial ground and the burials of the townsfolk had been placed in the grounds to the north side of the abbey post-dissolution. These burials therefore represent a previously unknown cemetery, probably created at the same time the church came into service in the early 15th century, and it may have ceased functioning as a burial ground about the time of the Dissolution in the first half of the 16th century.

It should be noted that Cross Street, which joins the south side of Church Street and was formerly known as Dead Man's Lane, is aligned with the area that was once the cemetery, and may have derived this name from being the common route from which many of the arrivals to the burial ground would have come.

The landscape around the church not only sloped down from west to east, but it also had a gradient from the north to the south, towards the river, with a fall in ground level of at least 1m. An effort was made to make the area more level, probably related to the construction of Butchers Row. This involved lowering the ground level on the north side of the cemetery which appears to have removed all evidence of any further graves. Some of the shallower burials were also truncated by a recent service trench and the modern churchyard wall.

None of the burials were lifted as they still lay in consecrated ground, and the church requested them to be left undisturbed. Each of the burials was covered in a sheet of permeable construction material, before being sealed with a layer of soil. They were then enclosed in concrete and slabs to protect them from the new construction work. The cemetery probably extended to the east side of Queen Street and between Exchange Street and Church Street, an area of approximately 600m².

Church Street

A trench to the south of the church revealed a street level probably contemporary with the construction of the church. It was composed of a roughly metalled road and path separated by large upright stone slabs that formed a kerb, adjacent to the south churchyard wall. A single sherd of Bourne B ware pottery of 13th to 15th century date was recovered from the path (Figs 3.14 and 3.15).

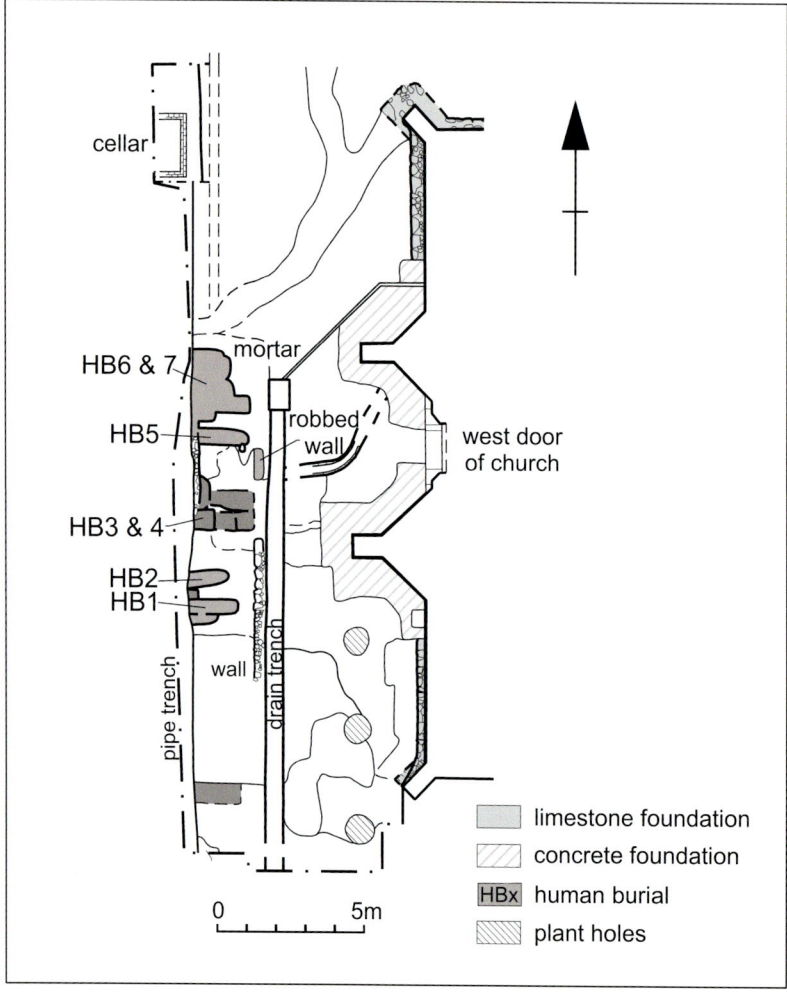

Fig 3.11: Churchyard burials to the west of the church

The post-medieval Cathedral Square (late 15th-17th centuries)

Following the Dissolution the abbey church was converted to cathedral status in 1541. The cathedral retained the governance over its own precincts, but the market square and the care and maintenance of the streets, now came under the jurisdiction of new secular governing body, the Feoffees.

Building in the south-east corner of Cathedral Square

With the change in authority responsible for the administration of public areas in the 16th century, a period of secular building was undertaken in the market square, which is illustrated in the John Speed map of 1610. It comprised the construction of a large rectangular building, Building 3, in the south-east corner of the square and a row of tenements to the west of the church (Fig 3.6)

The building illustrated in the south-east corner of the market square, as shown on Speed's map (Fig 2.3) survived as a series of fragmentary lengths of stone walls aligned either east-west or north-south, with areas of floor surfaces also surviving. The building was rectangular, measuring 25m east-west by 15m north-south (Figs 3.16, 3.17 and 3.18). Dumped pottery, probably from the building, recovered from the silting on the earliest pavement on its north side, would indicate a mid to late 15th-century construction date.

The structure may have consisted of a series of small shops along the north and south sides. The interior of the buildings displayed mortar and sand/clay beaten floors, with frontages and narrow internal partition walls between the rooms. One of the stone walls had a brick-lined threshold, possibly between rooms and

Fig 3.12: The skull of burial HB1

Fig 3.13: The femurs of burial HB6 overlying the feet of one or two earlier burials, HB7

FIG 3.14: KERB STONES EDGING A PATHWAY OF THE 15TH CENTURY, AGAINST THE STONE CHURCHYARD WALL (RIGHT), WITH THE ROAD (LEFT) AT A LOWER LEVEL, TRENCH 6

a possible door jamb was also observed. Remains of wall plaster were recovered from floor surfaces. Pottery from the floors and the yard area suggests occupation during the late 15th to 17th centuries. Other finds from the building included a pair of shears and a cloth seal (Fig 4.6, 16) and a possible waste deposit of crown glass may indicate that a variety of trades were being undertaken within the various tenements.

Street surfaces and paths

Throughout the life of the early market square surface, localised maintenance and repairs were undertaken. In association with Building 3, a pitched or slab stone pavement and street surface was laid on the north and west sides of the building, but did not appear to extend to the larger part of the square (Fig 3.19). The path, about 1.5m wide, flanked the north and west sides of the building, but which probably continued around its entire perimeter. To the north of the building several resurfacing events raised the street level, possibly as a response of the continuing accumulations of the dark silt, which continued into the 17th century.

Street monument: The market cross?

To the west of Building 3 there were the remains of a structure that was probably circular or polygonal in plan, with a diameter of *c.*5.0m. At ground level the edge of the feature had a low stone step or kerb set on the market square surface, although on its east side there was a pitched stone street and path.

Inside the stone step was a make-up layer or packing of limestone rubble. At the approximate centre of the feature there was a pile of roughly-laid ashlar blocks and at least one piece of fine moulded stonework dating from the late 13th to early 14th centuries, likely derived from the demolition of the 'old' parish church or the Chapel of St Thomas the Martyr (Thomas Becket). Overlying the stone was a deposit of gravel and a soil and rubble dump, forming a mound at least 1m high. This feature may have been the plinth for the market cross mentioned in town books of 1614 and 1649, but it had apparently disappeared by 1699. The date of its construction is unclear, but the first documentary evidence of a market cross appears to be from the early 15th century (Fig 3.20). The soil mound appears to have remained as a

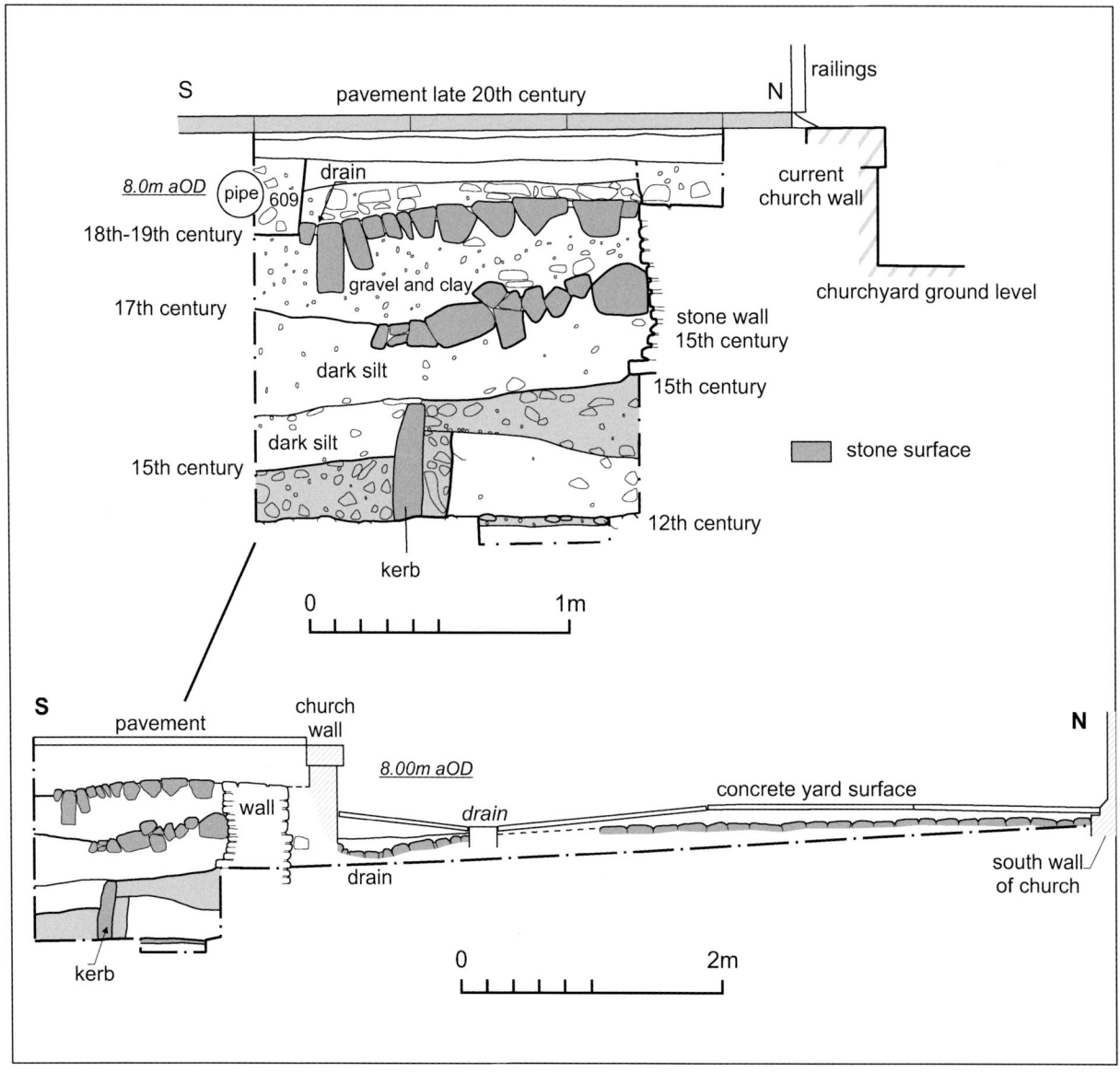

FIG 3.15: THE PAVEMENT SURFACES IN CHURCH STREET FROM THE 12TH TO 20TH CENTURIES (TOP) AND THE PAVEMENTS IN RELATION TO THE SUNKEN CHURCHYARD (BOTTOM)

feature in the square since the street silting was allowed to accumulate against and partly over it.

Butchers Row

To accommodate the new church and its churchyard, much of the space used by the butchers, probably including livestock pens, from at least the mid-13th century (Mackreth 1994) would have been taken over, leaving less space for stalls, but perhaps particularly for livestock pens.

John Speed's map of 1610 shows no indication of a cemetery, but illustrates an established row of tenements, arranged north-south lying immediately adjacent to the west of the parish church, known as Butchers Row. Clearly there had been a change in land use with the closure of the cemetery which was sealed by limestone rubble and a soil layer 0.10m to 0.30m deep, dating from the mid-16th to 17th centuries. The abandonment of the cemetery may relate to the 16th-century Reformation.

When the Butchers Row was first constructed the premises were probably commercial in use and, as the name denotes, they were all or partly connected with the butchers' trade. On the Eyres map of 1721 (Fig 2.5) the building at the north end of Butchers Row extended into the churchyard, and was known to be the premises of the church sexton. It is possible that since the church was located in the square, the north-east corner of the cemetery had always been occupied by the Sexton's House, which would have been the ideal location, as his job included being the town's gravedigger. This may also be why the northern part of the churchyard contained no extant burials.

3. The Archaeology of Cathedral Square

Fig 3.16: The fountain array area with the two deeper trenches containing walls and floors of Building 3, looking north-east

The demise of the 'row' began in the later part of the 19th century with the removal of the buildings at its southern end for the enlargement of the Corn Exchange. The north end of the 'row', including the Sexton's House, survived until the end of the 19th century when the building was demolished for the final extension of the Corn Exchange.

Although Butchers Row was well-recorded in documentary and cartographic evidence, few physical remains survived. There was a small area of three or four overlying room surfaces of clay and mortar, in the location of the Sexton's House. Contemporary with the earliest clay floor was a broken decorated medieval stone mortar, 0.40m in diameter, set into the natural gravel. It had a hole in its base with a slate roof tile underneath it, with a green cess-like silt accumulation around the base of the bowl suggesting it had been reused as a urinal. The mortar had been backfilled with ash before it was sealed below a later clay floor, with a final floor of lime mortar above this (Figs 3.21 and 3.22).

The outline of the Sexton's building in the churchyard may have been defined by the remains of a flagstone path in the churchyard, but no remains of the building had survived (Fig 3.23).

Dark organic silts

Although the building and resurfacing had been undertaken in parts of the square, dark silt continued to accumulate in the main open area of the square and the streets surrounding it.

The Guildhall and the redevelopment of the square (late 17th century)

The Guildhall

Through most of the 17th century little obvious change occurred around the area of the market square, the Civil War and the Commonwealth appear to have had little effect on the secular environment of Peterborough. It was not until late in the century, with the restoration of Charles II, that the there was any public and political will to improve the conditions of the city centre streets, where dark silt waste had continued to accumulate.

This development created a marked change in the look of the square, with the construction of the Guildhall forming the centre piece, a public building consisting of a large chamber supported on open arches, forming a

FIG 3.17: EXTANT STONE WALL OF BUILDING 3 (FOREGROUND) WITH ROBBED WALL AND FLOORS BEHIND, LOOKING NORTH

FIG 3.18: BUILDING 3, THE EAST WALL, FOREGROUND, AND NARROW INTERNAL WALLS AND FLOORS BEHIND, BUILT OVER THE LEVELLED REMAINS OF BUILDING 1, LOOKING WEST

FIG 3.19: PAVEMENT AND STREET SURFACE ON THE WEST SIDE OF BUILDING 3

covered market space. A public subscription was started in 1669, with the completion of the structure in 1671, which in its formative years was known as the Chamber over the Cross. It was located in the market square to the east side of the church (Figs 3.24 and 3.25).

Adjacent to the east side of the Guildhall, there was a 3.0m length of curving stone foundation, probably part of an estimated 17m-diameter circular base on which the building is probably supported. The foundations were approximately 0.5m deep, constructed on a similar depth of clay and cornbrash rubble make-up overlying the dark silt deposit (Fig 3.26).

The construction of the Guildhall almost certainly replaced the Butter Cross that had been established in the square as a covered market at least from the early 1600s. It is shown on the John Speed map of 1610 (Fig 2.3) as a circular or polygonal building, together with a tall circular structure, which was also probably removed during this phase of development.

Resurfacing of the square

To escape the dire conditions created by the dark silt, the square and the streets levels were raised and resurfaced

3. The Archaeology of Cathedral Square

Fig 3.20: Remains of the 15th-16th-century street monument in Cathedral Square

Fig 3.21: Stone mortar set in the floor of building on Butchers Row, possibly to use as a urinal

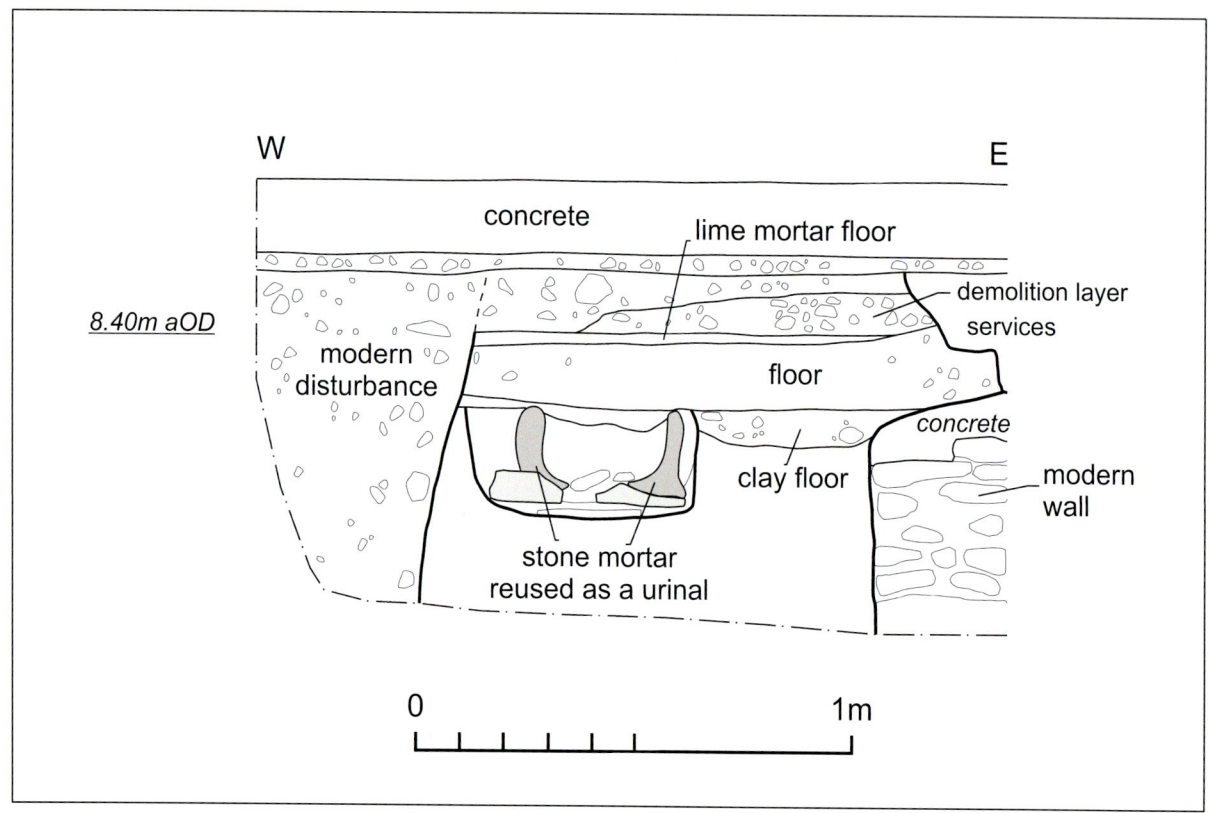

Fig 3.22: The Sexton's house, floor layers and possible urinal in section

Fig 3.23: Flagstones at west end of churchyard may outline the location of the Sexton's house at the north end of Butchers Row, looking south towards the surviving burgage tenement buildings on Church Street

in stone. A large quantity of cornbrash rubble and clay was brought into the square, raising the ground level to between 0.5m to 1.0m above the dark silt level. The make-up material displayed distinct tip lines from west to east, with the greatest depth to the west becoming shallower to the east. Overlying the make-up deposits was a surface of compacted small to medium, sub-angular limestone chips and fragments with the upper surface worn through use. The surface exhibited a slight incline to the east side of the square to encourage drainage, so as to negate the possibility of further silt accumulations on the square. The ground did rise towards the Guildhall, but a fairly level area was formed on its east side, possibly to accommodate the weekly market.

The resurfacing appears to have been fairly extensive as it was observed in Church Street (Fig 3.15), up to Queen Street and Cowgate and in Cumbergate, directly overlying the dark silt. It was probably during the raising of the ground level and resurfacing that Building 3, in the south-west corner of the square was demolished. Although there was no direct evidence, the remains of the building were probably sealed by the new surface.

Churchyard pitched-stone surface

The street and square improvement scheme appears to have included the churchyard with the introduction of a surface of pitched stone, gently tipping from the church wall to an open, pitched-stone drain adjacent to

3. The Archaeology of Cathedral Square

Fig 3.24: The Guildhall in 1896, looking west, showing the row of buildings between the Guildhall and the church

Fig 3.25: The eastern façade of the Guildhall

33

Fig 3.26: Guildhall stone foundations in fountain drain trench on the east side of the building, Guildhall to right, looking south-west

the churchyard wall. The surface was only present in the south-eastern part of the churchyard; the other areas had undoubtedly been truncated and levelled by later activity.

Church Street pavement

A pitched-stone path 1.0m wide ran along the length of the churchyard wall on the north side of Church Street (Figs 3.15 and 3.27). The path had a slight incline into the street that had lost its stone surface exposing the dark silt deposit beneath. It is possible the churchyard wall may have been reconstructed at the same time or at some stage post-dating the laying of the pitched surfaces, as the wall appears to be slightly offset to the south at the new ground level.

Queen Street

To the west of the parish church, at the south end of Queen Street, there was a base of a possible drain aligned east-west, 1.5m long by 0.15m wide. It was composed of rectangular blocks with a flat upper surface. The upper part of the drain had probably been removed as the stone base was overlaid by recent make-up material. Although no date for the drain was produced, the underlying deposit of dark silt deposit contained 16th-century Cistercian ware pottery, which makes the drain probably part of the resurfacing of the 17th century or later.

Surface silts

The problem of the silting in the eastern part of the market square appears to have been resolved by the remodelling, as only a thin layer of silt was observed, possibly as a result of the sloping of the surface, but also due to possible cleaning and maintenance. However, dark organic silt accumulated to the west of the parish church, in the north part of the square, centred on Butchers Row, which included Queen Street, Church Street, Cowgate and Cumbergate, as a deposit 0.20m thick (Fig 3.28). The continuing presence of the dark silt in these streets was probably due to their location in the area of the well-established butcher's market that still produced an excess of waste material.

The churchyard escaped the worst of the street silting as it was enclosed by a wall, although it did accumulate some silt over the pitched-stone surface, especially in the open drain.

Redevelopment of Cathedral Square (late 18th early 19th centuries)

During the 120 years from the time of the construction of the Guildhall and the resurfacing of the market square, the main development was the construction of a row of buildings between the Church of St John the Baptist and adjoining the west side of the Guildhall, as pictured on

Fig 3.27: Pitched-stone path of the 17th century, overlaid by a pitched-stone pavement of the late 18th to early 19th century, both abutting the churchyard stone wall (right), looking west

the Eyre's map of 1721 (Fig 2.5). A short length of stone wall, aligned north to south, and a small area of brick-laid surface, located between the church and the Guildhall are probably remains from these early buildings, grouped as Building 5, but probably elements of more than one phase of works largely lost to later developments. The map also displayed Butchers Row, with the Sexton's House at the north end, extending into the churchyard. To the west of Butchers Row the map shows a new block of buildings separated by a narrow lane and alleyway.

The waste clogged streets of Peterborough appeared to still have been a major problem at the end of the 18th century, probably due to the neglect of the Feoffees, the authority responsible for the maintenance of the roads. In 1789 the Feoffees were relieved of their responsibilities and in 1790 the Peterborough Pavement and Improvement Commission was established. The Commission was enacted to clear the thoroughfares and resurface the streets.

Resurfacing of the square

The 17th-century market square surface appeared to be intact and still in use in the late 18th century, with little surface silting, but the adjacent streets were in a state of disorder from the accumulation of waste. The new commission was established in part due to these conditions with the power to rectify it. The new authority appears to have made a decision to undertake a similar process to the late 17th-century construction, by raising the square and street level and resurfacing.

Limestone cornbrash and clay make-up deposits were dumped onto the central market square area in front of the Guildhall with a surface, overall, gently tipping east. The make-up deposits were overlaid by a gravel sub-base 0.2m to 0.4m thick. Into the gravel sub-base was set a substantial surface of pitched limestone slabs aligned north-south, with shallow open gullies/drains, 0.5m wide, of pitched limestone set east-west, to facilitate drainage to the east. This surface was observed as truncated areas in the southern part of Cathedral Square, but it can be assumed it was a much more extensive surface throughout the square and the adjacent streets (Fig 3.29). A largely intact length of the pitched-stone path and drain lay along the side of Church Street, adjacent to the churchyard, undisturbed by recent buried services (Figs 3.30-3.32).

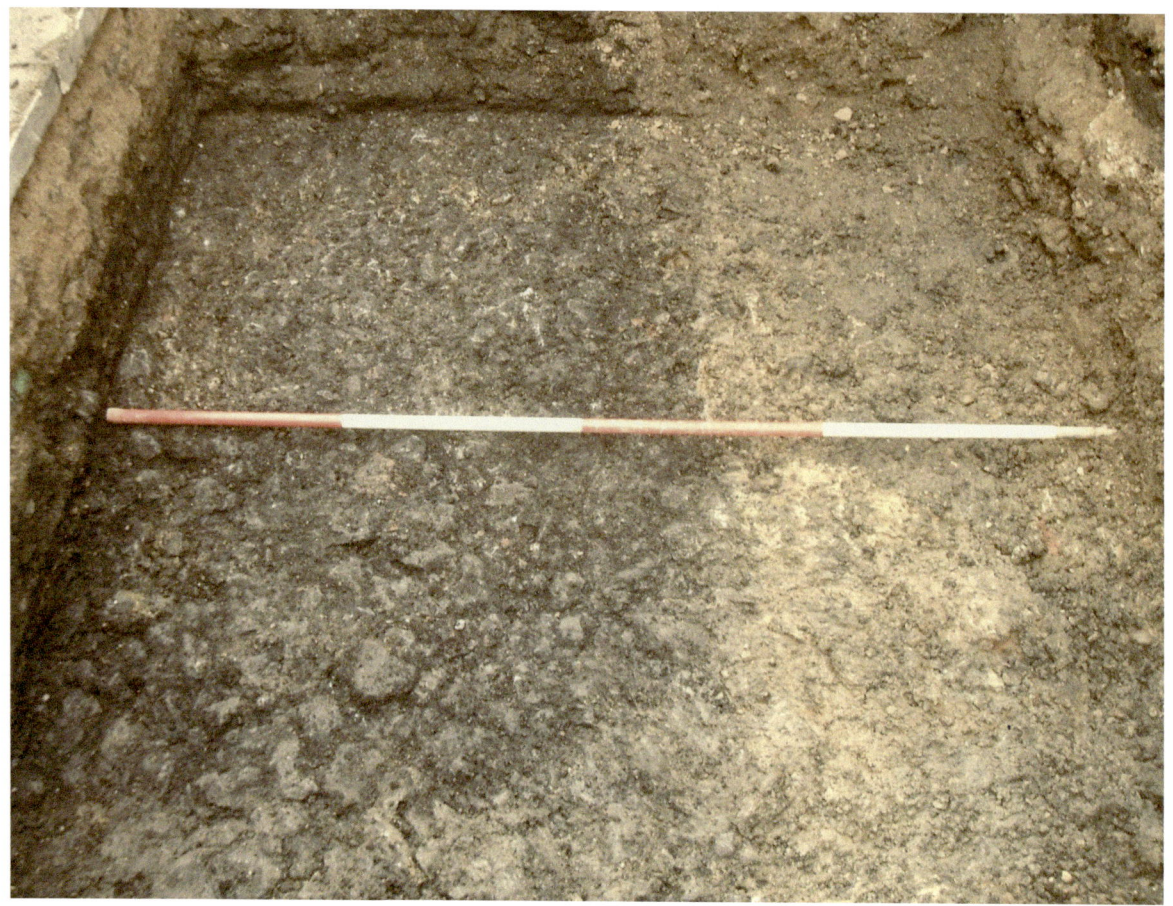

Fig 3.28: Street surface of the 17th century, overlaid by the dark silt, cut by a modern pipe trench to the right, Queen Street, looking south

Fig 3.29: Pitched-stone surface of the late 18th- to early 19th centuries, with underlying make-up layers, sealing the dark silt under Cathedral Square in the east, looking north

3. The Archaeology of Cathedral Square

FIG 3.30: PITCHED-STONE PAVEMENT WITH AN OPEN GUTTER ALONG ITS OUTER EDGE, TO THE SOUTH OF THE CHURCH, CUT BY A VICTORIAN BRICK CULVERT, LOOKING EAST

The records suggest the market area and the street surfaces had the 'cobbled' pitched-stone surface, with footpaths of flagstones edged with kerbs. The only flagstones identified that were still in use were within the churchyard, forming pavements in front of the north, south and west entrances to the church, including an area in the north-west corner of the churchyard that may have been a path around the Sexton's House. It is not known if these were the original locations of the flagstones, but even if that was the case, they appear to have been re-laid on recent make up deposits.

Sometime subsequent to introduction of the make-up layers and gravel, the remains of Building 3 in the south-east corner of the square were further robbed out, with some of the gravel filling the robber trench before it was backfilled. The robbing of the walls may have occurred at a later date, but recent truncation by the A15 road has removed all the earlier surfaces.

Surface silts

The introduction of gutters and probably street maintenance as well, seems to have kept the thoroughfares and square clear and accessible, with accumulation of only a few centimetres of silts, but increasing to 150mm in parts of the open gutters.

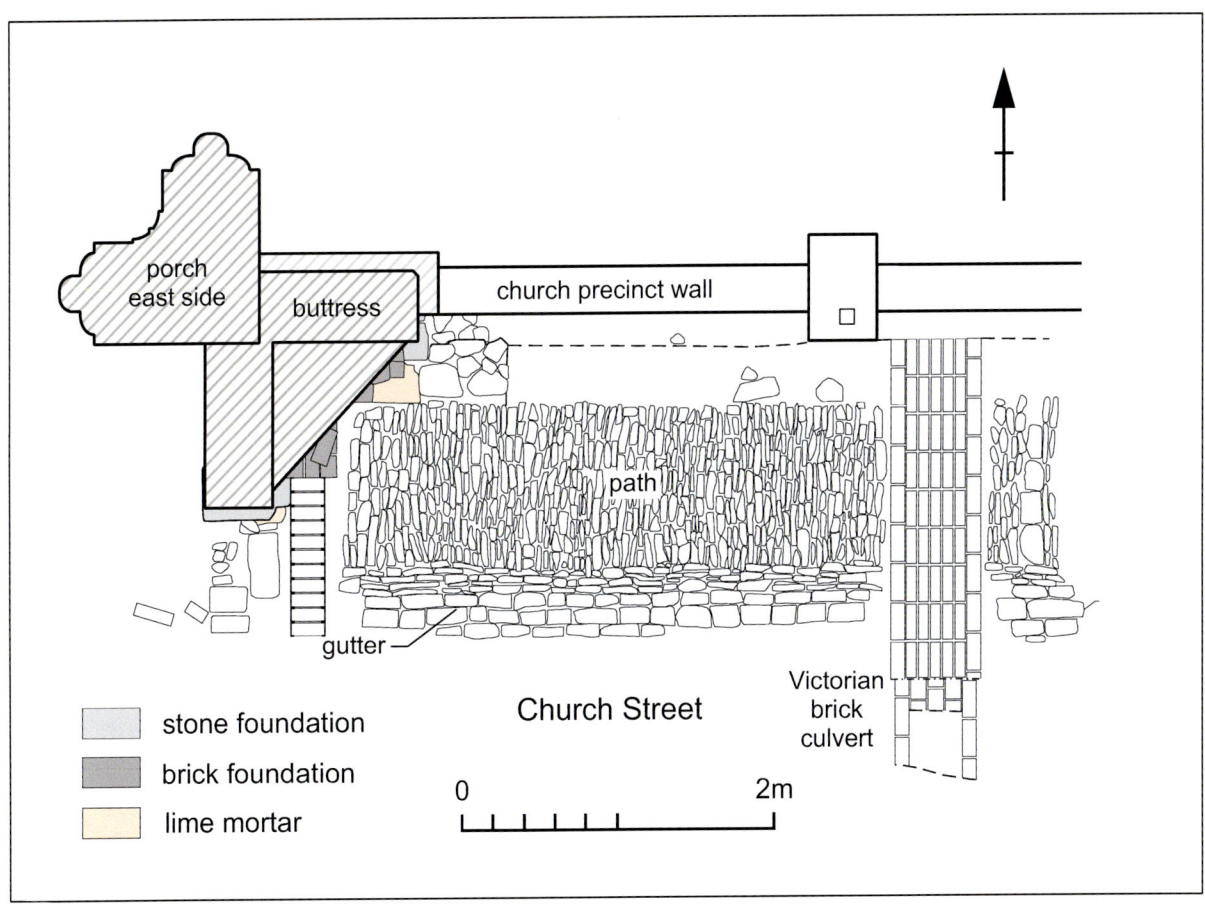

FIG 3.31: PITCHED-STONE PAVEMENT OF THE 18TH CENTURY, CUT BY A BRICK CULVERT OF THE 19TH CENTURY, SOUTH OF THE CHURCH

The History and Archaeology of Cathedral Square Peterborough

FIG 3.32: PAVEMENT AT THE EAST END OF THE CHURCHYARD WALL, LOOKING WEST

The modern square (19th-20th centuries)

Peterborough in the 19th century saw a period of growth and expansion for the city, especially with the arrival of the railways in the middle part of the century. This was reflected in the commercial centre, with new building development in and around Cathedral Square. The changes were partly due to the response of the local government, initially the Improvements Commission, but this authority was replaced by the Municipal Borough Council in 1874.

By the 19th century probably little remained of the early burgage tenement blocks, as the new larger commercial and public premises now dominated the street frontages. However, two 17th-century buildings still exist on the south side of the square (Fig 3.33).

The products of progress and development in the 19th century were observed in the excavations throughout Cathedral Square and adjacent streets. The remains of commercial and public buildings were recorded between the Guildhall and the Church of St John the Baptist, to the west side of the church, on Bridge Street, Cumbergate, Cowgate, Queen Street, and Exchange Street. Changes were also taking place around the church with the replacement of the churchyard wall. In the Market Square

FIG 3.33: BUILDINGS OF THE 17TH CENTURY SURVIVING ON CHURCH STREET, LOOKING SOUTH

and the streets, not only was there new street surfacing, but Victorian engineering was coming to the fore with the introduction of gas mains, water pipes, and a series of brick culverts for street drainage, all concealed as buried services.

Buildings between the parish church and the Guildhall

This area was the site of many buildings from at least the 17th century through to the 20th centuries. A length of stone wall to the south was a rare surviving element of an early building, and an area of brick floor was part of a later building, both listed as Building 5 (Fig 3.34). There were more substantial remains of stone and brick foundations and cellarage of several of the later buildings (Buildings 6, 7 and 8; Figs 3.34-3.36). The buildings at the northern end of the row, Buildings 7 and 6, were photographed in the late 19th century (Fig 3.24).

The north side had also been heavily truncated by a 20th-century subterranean toilet block, although the foundations on the west and south side of the earlier buildings may have been partly utilised in the modern walls.

The Corn Exchange

The area to the west of the church was dominated by the presence of the 1960s Norwich Union Building, a concrete tower block, until its demolition as part of the new development. Due to its scale it largely removed all evidence of previous activity, although some significant remains of the previous standing building, the Corn Exchange, did survive. Although, as they shared a similar footprint, what the 20th-century building did not remove was probably already truncated by the Corn Exchange itself, apart from the remains of possibly the Sexton's House mentioned above.

With the demolition of the Norwich Union Building and the landscaping of the area for the new St John's Square, remnants of the Corn Exchange were uncovered. There were lengths of concrete and brick foundations, especially around the east corner, up to 1.5m deep, but the best preserved part of the building was in the north-east corner, where part of the white glazed brick walls and a diagonal chequer board tiled floor (red and black) of the subterranean toilet area was located, 1.3m below the existing street level (Fig 3.37). The toilet area was probably part of the final 1893 extension of the building.

Bridge Street (Narrow Bridge Street)

Before the present Bridge Street was widened in the 1930s by demolishing the east side frontages, it was a much narrower thoroughfare, hence its earlier name, Narrow (Bridge) Street. Only the north end of the street lay within the development, in the very south-east corner of Cathedral Square. In front of the present NatWest Bank building there was the remains of a short length of a brick and a limestone ashlar wall. This may represent the back walls of two adjacent building that once faced onto Narrow Street. The east side of the walls were abutted by a possible garden or yard soil. No dating evidence was recovered, but the buildings were likely to be either 19th or early 20th-century construction.

Cumbergate

This street now forms a short thoroughfare from Exchange Street to the entrance of the Queensgate shopping centre, which supplanted the part of the street that originally formed a dog-leg and joined the Long Causeway. The modern street development has made an incursion into the surviving east side of Cumbergate, up to a building frontage, presently used as tearooms, but originally erected as almshouses by the Feoffees in 1903, from a fund bequeathed to the city by a Miss Frances Pears.

The street area in front of the building was the Almshouses garden, walled off from Cumbergate, of which a 14m length of the foundations, aligned approximately south-west to north-east, with street and building frontage survives (Figs 2.6, 2.7 and 3.38). Adjacent to the east side of the wall was a short 2.0m length of stone wall. Although this has been attributed an early medieval date, it may be part of the probably 18th- or 19th-century almshouses that fronted the street. A remnant of a garden soil and a possible bedding feature was present to the east side of the wall.

There was a disturbed stone cobble street surface, cut by the wall foundations, from which 17th- or 18th-century pottery was recovered.

Exchange Street

Trench 12, in Exchange Street, contained a part of a possible cellar wall composed of clay-bonded limestone blocks, probably replaced by a recent reinforced concrete cellar most likely associated with the commercial property on the south-west corner of Cumbergate and Exchange Street.

Queen Street, 18th-century townhouse

On the west side of Queen Street stands a brick town house of quality from the mid-18th century, with a central Venetian window and entrance. It is presently in use as a public house, The Grapevine (Fig 3.39), though not the historical Grapevine public house, now gone, which was on a different site. The reduction in the street level and the excavation of the service trenches prior to the new resurfacing gave opportunity to record the foundations of the building, and a partly obscured wall cavity for a boot scraper, adjacent to the north side of the entrance. The presence of a boot scraper in the 18th-century city centre appears to be a clear indictment to the

Fig 3.34: Buildings between the parish church and the Guildhall

3. THE ARCHAEOLOGY OF CATHEDRAL SQUARE

FIG 3.35: WEST OF THE GUILDHALL, A STAIRWELL WITH STEPS DOWN TO THE CELLAR THRESHOLD, BUILDING 8, CELLAR 4,

FIG 3.36: NORTH-WEST OF THE GUILDHALL, STONE CELLAR WALL AND BRICK FLOOR, BUILDING 7, CELLAR 2,

conditions of the pavements at this late date, even after all the previous street improvements.

Cowgate trench

As part of the development a new electric sub-station was located in Cowgate between properties 8 and 10 on the south side of the street, 37m from the street frontage and 4m from the rear of the shared tenement plot boundary with residences of neighbouring Priestgate. From the sub-station a trench for the cable ducts was excavated down an alleyway to the street frontage. The alleyway lay north-south, square to the street frontage, which was probably first recorded on the 1821 enclosure map, but the later maps show the frontage covering the alleyway as it is today.

A possible buried soil overlying the natural clay, was encountered close the frontage of Cowgate with a gradual fall to the south, consistent with the drop in the natural layers across the square towards the river. No dating evidence was recovered. Overlying these deposits was a mixed make-up/levelling layer composed of demolition debris, possibly from previous buildings that occupied the site, creating a level building surface at the Cowgate frontage. The pottery recovered from this deposit is dated to the 19th century.

Beyond the building frontages the alleyway widened and opened into a yard area. This area, until probably recent times, had been occupied by a probable 19th- or 20th-century building, now demolished. From the demolished building in the south to the end of the trench was occupied by a dark grey garden soil up to 0.4m deep, containing 19th-20th-century pottery.

Overlying the layers was either brick or coarse orange-brown gravel, forming a track or yard surface. In the 19th century, they probably formed an alleyway path or yard level, which was fairly level throughout its length

Fig 3.37: Corn exchange; remains of wall and floor of the subterranean toilet, looking east

Fig 3.38: Miss Pears' almshouses, looking north east, with garden brick wall foundations (foreground)

Fig 3.39: An 18th-century town house on Queen Street, now The Grapevine public house, looking west from Exchange Street

at 0.40m to 0.60m below the existing surface, though it became slightly shallower at the Cowgate frontage with a depth of 0.3m, where the bricks were overlaid by tarmac. The surfaces were sealed by recent dark grey clay loam make-up layer up to 0.5m thick, containing 19th-century pottery and clay tobacco-pipe. The existing surface was composed of an established brick and stone slab surface in the alleyway with a more recent concrete and brick surface in the southern yard area.

Church of St John the Baptist

The church structure went through some considerable change in the 19th century, as it originally had a spire that had to be removed in the 1820s when it was deemed to be unsafe. This was probably part of the work undertaken between 1819 and 1820, by the St John's Act of Parliament granted in 1819. In the 1880s the building went through further extensive restoration work (Bull and Bull 2007).

In the latter part of the century the medieval stone churchyard wall was demolished and replaced, with a 'new' low wall topped by wrought iron railings, opening up the lower part of the church to street view. The new wall extended around the entire churchyard with the exception of four new entrances comprising stone clad plinths and iron gateways. Stone steps led from these entrances into the churchyard (Figs 3.40 and 3.41).

Part of the early work included the existing lead downpipes of the church, which were officially marked 1819 on their chute outlets at the roof level. Some of the pipes at the churchyard level displayed interesting graffiti. The handiwork including people's initials, surnames, decorated gloves and a figure wearing top hat and tails in a pugilist pose, including a date of 1831. The graffiti appears to have been created by scoring or a succession of indents from the point of a knife (Fig 3.42).

Victorian services

Remains of buried Victorian services engineering was present in many of the trenches throughout the square in the form of gas mains/water pipes, and a series of brick culverts for street drainage, now redundant and, more often or not, truncated by more recent services (Figs 3.43 and 3.44). Much of these services were probably contemporary with the laying of the granite sett surface in Cathedral Square and throughout adjoining streets, which was largely due to the impetus from the growth of industry and the population of Peterborough in the late 19th century. The planning and construction of these

FIG 3.40: CHURCH GATEWAY, NORTH-WEST CORNER OF THE CHURCHYARD, LOOKING NORTH ONTO EXCHANGE STREET

FIG 3.41: CHURCHYARD RAILINGS ON THE NORTH SIDE OF THE CHURCH

public services was the responsibility of the Municipal Borough Council, established in 1874.

The most complex and far-reaching of the subterranean services excavated was the brick drainage culvert system, present in most of the thoroughfares around Cathedral Square. The effect of the this comprehensive network of drainage culverts was to prevent surface water developing and washing away silt and other debris off the streets, creating a cleaner and more habitable environment in the city centre.

In most cases, the culverts appeared as a brick barrel-vaulted drain at least at least 0.5m high and up to 0.6m wide, with vertical sides and a brick base. They were placed in trenches no less than one metre below ground level, either side of the street, close to the street drainage gutters, probably containing down gullies into the culvert, although only one possible example of this was found in Cowgate.

Where they were identified in Cowgate, Church Street and Exchange Street, the culverts were aligned approximately east-west, parallel with the streets. Shallower culverts were identified coming out of the churchyard, most likely for the outflow of the church

3. The Archaeology of Cathedral Square

Fig 3.42: Graffiti on 19th-century lead pipes on the church of St John the Baptist: showing a name, GRAIL, and a date of 1831 (left), and a figure in top hat and tails in a pugilist pose (right)

downpipes off its roof, which then probably joined the Church Street drain. At the south end of the Long Causeway the side of a culvert, orientated north-south was located in the section of a trench and from its external shape it was probably circular or oval in cross-section. It would seem most likely that the culverts aligned east-west joined the north-south ones, which probably then continued down Bridge Street opening out into the river.

Granite street surface

The last of the surfaces to be laid before the pavements and roads of the 20th century, was an extensive level surface of granite setts, small roughly-shaped sub-rectangular blocks, replacing the pitched-stone surface of the late 18th-century. This surface was only identified *in situ* in two small areas, one on the north side of the square, close to the toilet block, the other below the Cathedral West Gate (Fig 3.45). Pictorial evidence suggests this surface was constructed in the 1870s, which was probably the responsibility of the Municipal Borough Council, the newly created city authority in 1874. The surface appears to have been laid throughout the square and the neighbouring streets. Similar views photographed in 1919 show the granite sett surface had been sealed below tarmacadam, which was evident from the surviving surfaces.

It is possible some of the upper make-up layers attributed to the 18th-century surface, where it had been removed, may relate to levelling the ground for the granite sett surface, as the date for these layers could not always be determined, but they were unlikely to be substantial deposits, with the deepest to the east to compensate where the greatest fall in ground level occurred.

Fig 3.43: Victorian brick culvert on the north side of Church Street, cutting a pitched-stone pavement of the late 18th to early 19th century

The make-up layers laid prior to the granite setts comprised a firm layer of dark coloured grit and gravel with silty/sandy clay matrix, including limestone fragments. The layer was 0.04m to 0.20m deep. It

Fig 3.44: Excavated section through culvert, looking north

was identified as an extensive but patchy layer across Cathedral Square, along Church Street and possibly as far as Cowgate. Although the granite sett surface had been removed by later activity, granite setts occasionally appeared in disturbed layers and backfills.

Photographs also show an elaborate lamp-post in Cathedral Square, and this was replaced by the Gates Memorial in 1897. The memorial was a fountain which honoured Henry Pearson Gates, the city's first mayor. Although the monument was removed to Bishop's Road gardens in 1963, the concrete foundations remained, occupying an area of 5-6m2 and at least 0.7m thick, in the location of the northern array of fountains.

Development in the 20th century

Major development and changes, throughout the area of investigation, began in the 1930s with the demolition of Narrow Street for the creation of the broader thoroughfare of Bridge Street and the building of the new City Hall.

The main road routes, the A15 and A47, now also passed through the city centre, along Long Causeway, Church Street, Cowgate and Bridge Street, making it the hub of the local transport network. The A15 and A47 were major trunk roads before the motorways were built, with the A47 forming the main east-west route across the country from Norwich to Leicester and the A15 the north road to Lincoln, both passing through Peterborough. With the new 1930s development of the city centre, it must have been considered appropriate to encourage new business and trade to the city by redirecting the main roads through it. The A47 approached from the west by Cowgate, along Church Street and up the Long Causeway, with the A15 passing through newly widened Bridge Street, leading to Westgate to join the Lincoln Road. These main roads linked directly with Exchange Street, Queen Street and Cross Street, including Cumbergate.

Fig 3.45: Remnant granite setts of the late 19th to early 20th century, under the Cathedral's West Gate, looking south

The road building would have a significant effect on Cathedral Square layout and the adjacent streets, with the increase in motor traffic, and consequently the reduction in the public space, with a smaller area for the market. The construction of the new roads resulted in the largely stripping away of the 19th-century granite sett surface, but the earlier stone surfaces and features were affected to a lesser extent, as they were preserved by their greater depth of burial. Evidence for the mid-20th century road system, could be seen in many of the trenches across at the east end of the square, from the south end of the Long Causeway to the north end of Bridge Street, with roads leading off the main roads through the Great Gate and north up Exchange Street.

In the later part of the 20th century, in 1963, the market was moved from Cathedral Square to the old cattle market on the north side of City Road, bringing to an end its original function after about 800 years. The Gates monument was also moved, making the square a more open public area.

In 1964 the Corn Exchange was demolished, with the construction of the Norwich Union Building replacing it and opening in 1966. Underground toilets and an electricity substation were located between the church of St John the Baptist and the Guildhall, in the area formerly occupied by the 18th to 19th-century buildings. Early 20th-century underpinning of the tower of St John the

3. The Archaeology of Cathedral Square

Fig 3.46: Present day Cathedral Square, with the new fountain arrays in use, looking east towards the Cathedral's West Gate

Baptist was also recorded (Walker 2010). In Cathedral Square a fountain was constructed in the early 1960s, which was in recent times replaced by a pair of circular flowerbeds (Figs 2.2 and 2.4).

During the 1960s, the streets and paths were repaved with a mixture of concrete slabs and herring-bone laid block paved road surfaces. The Yorkshire flagstones were arranged around the Cathedral Gate and the NatWest Bank, in keeping with the stone buildings, with the surface leading into the more modern concrete pavements of Cathedral Square and Bridge Street. It should be noted that none of the existing pavements or road surface throughout the area of investigation were dated any earlier than the mid to late 20th century, apart from possibly the flagstone surfaces within the churchyard of St John the Baptist, which may be 18th or 19th century in date.

The major development of the Queensgate Shopping Centre in the late 1970s to the north side of Cathedral Square did not directly affect it, but it changed the adjacent street plan, especially the medieval street of Cumbergate. It almost entirely disappeared under the development, except for a length of the southern arm that leads into Exchange Street, which became pedestrianised.

The excavated evidence of development through the 20th-century was present as multiple service trenches, street furniture foundations of bollards and sign posts, extensive buried remains of the road make-up layers of tarmac and concrete. The square and the neighbouring streets were laid with paving slabs and brick road surfaces.

Multiple drainage and utility services were encountered throughout the area of investigation, mainly at the periphery of the square and along the street frontages to serve the shops and commercial premises. The open area strip across the development area involved the removal of the pavement and road surfaces and underlying make-up deposits and backfill, exposing many of the utilities (electricity and power cables, communication ducts, etc), with the deeper buried utilities (drains, gas and water mains, etc), marked by service covers and inspection hatches.

Many of the deeper service pipes and cables were encountered in test trenches and excavations for new services, allowing keyhole views of the deeper buried archaeology. Not all the trenches excavated revealed archaeology, as only recent backfills and make-up layers were visible. Buried services were uncovered in all the trenches except Trench 31.

Date	Historical development	Archaeological features
7th-11th centuries	Saxon monastery and burh	Posthole, pit
12th-14th centuries	Great Fire of Peterborough, 1116 Rebuilding of the monastery First market square New town & market square, 1145 Cathedral gateway Stone bridge built over town ditch, 13th-14th centuries	Market square surface Dark organic silt first appears Building 1 (Cathedral Square) Cathedral Gateway foundations Stone wall and pit (Cumbergate) Dismantled (bridge?) ashlar blocks (near Cathedral Gate)
Late 14th-early 15th centuries	Demolition of 'old' parish church and part of the chapel of St Thomas the Martyr Consecration of the 'new' parish church of St John the Baptist, 1407	Cemetery west side of church Churchyard wall Road surface/path/kerb (Church Street) Market resurfacing and market cross
Late 15th-17th centuries	Dissolution of monastery, 1539 Creation of Peterborough Cathedral, 1541 Establishment of Feoffees, 1570s Speed's map, 1610 Butcher's Row first established	Building 3 (Cathedral Square) Resurface adjacent building (Cathedral Square) Internal floors Butchers Row Stone wall (south side toilet block) Street monument remains (Cathedral Square) Wall/drain capping (Queen Street) Walls (Cathedral Square, Cumbergate) Last organic silt deposit Levelling over cemetery and churchyard
Late 17th-18th centuries	The Restoration Construction of Guildhall, 1671 Eyre's map, 1722 Town house on Queen Street (public house, The Grapevine) Final infilling of town ditch	Demolition tenement block (Cathedral Square) Extensive make-up and resurfacing Churchyard pitched-stone surface New churchyard wall Surface silting Foundations and boot-scraper (The Grapevine)
Late 18th-19th centuries	Improvements and Pavements Commission, 1790 Theatre 1799-1846 Tenements between church & Guildhall Churchyard wall replaced by railings Lead down piping around church, 1818 Peterborough Enclosure map, 1821 Act of Incorporation, creation of Municipal Borough Council and Mayor, 1874 Demolition of Butchers Row for Corn Exchange 1848-1893 Mayor Gates Memorial erected 1897	Robbed-out tenement walls (Cathedral Square) Resurfacing and surface silting Cellars and foundations between church and Guildhall Victorian subterranean services Brick foundation and toilet basement of Corn Exchange Brick/stone wall (Bridge Street) Make-up layers (Cowgate Yard) Cellar wall (Exchange Street) Wall/drain (Queen Street) Granite setts (Cathedral Square and Gate) Concrete base (Gates Memorial) Base of telegraph pole
Early-mid 20th century	Redevelopment of Bridge Street, New City Hall, 1930s Main A15/47 roads through city centre	Wall foundations (Bridge Street) Wall improvements (Cathedral Gate) Tarmac surfaces, kerbs, etc A15/47 Concrete surface, flower beds John the Baptist churchyard
Late 20th century	Gates Memorial moved to Bishops Road gardens 1963 Corn Exchange demolished 1964 for Norwich Union building 1966 Underground toilets & substation Fountain early 1960s Queensgate development late 1970s Fountain replaced by flowerbeds 1980s	Concrete plinth Norwich Union Toilet block walls Fountain foundations Street furniture signatures Multiple service trenches Road construction Slab and brick pavements throughout

TABLE 3.1: SUMMARY OF CHRONOLOGY

4. The finds and environmental evidence

The following reports describe the pottery, other material finds, the animal bone and other environmental evidence, recovered during the excavations. Detailed tabulations of the finds and supplementary catalogues are available as an appendix to the client report (Morris 2016), which is available online through the Archaeology Data Service (ADS). Site context numbers (in brackets) have been retained for potential reference to the Appendices attached to the client report.

The pottery
by Iain Soden

The work on the trenches in Cathedral Square produced 1553 sherds of pottery, weighing 24.0kg from 150 contexts. The wider investigations produced a further 1384 sherds weighing 20.4kg from 130 contexts. All the pottery from each intervention has been taken into account.

As a whole, the assemblage comprises vessel fragments in 29 production types, ranging in date from the late 12th or early 13th centuries to the 19th century.

The pottery fabrics

In the absence of a widely accepted medieval and post-medieval type series for Peterborough, the nomenclature adopted remains that preferred for the published site of The Still (Spoerry and Hinman 1998). Most types are represented in the neighbouring Northamptonshire County Type series and it is to this that secondary recourse has also been made to aid identification. The Northamptonshire Type Series contains considerable numbers of sherds both from consumer sites and from the kilns of the surrounding industries represented here. The fabrics present are set out below in order of their broad chronological appearance and production date range (Table 4.1).

Residuality and the industries supplying the Market Square

There is little to suggest that any of the early material of 12th to early 15th century date is stratified. Most is residual in later features and deposits. Amongst this earlier material are sherds from the prominent industry in the Northamptonshire villages of Lyveden and its neighbour Stanion, excavated in the 1960s, early 1970s and 2002 (Foard 1991 and Chapman *et al* 2008). The early, type-A, shelly wares are part of a wider regional tradition going back to St Neots-type wares, but the hard grey and highly oolitic B fabric, under a strong green glaze, is very distinctive. Contemporary pottery has been noted from Thetford and Grimston, in Norfolk, but in very small quantities.

From the middle of the 15th century onwards, almost all of the interventions have been dominated by Bourne D ware, dated *c.*1450-1637. Far from reflecting any biased retrieval policy, this is a real domination of the market represented, being 52% of sherds and 65% by weight. In this, it is a broadly similar reliance on supply seen at The Still (Spoerry and Hinman 1998, 51 fig 16 and 71, 77) and later in 2001 at Cumbergate. The ware predominantly has the distinctive hard, fine orange-buff fabric and off-white surface slipping distinguishable (McCarthy and Brooks 1988, 409, 411). Represented here are jugs, bowls or basins, jars and cisterns with bung holes. Decoration is minimal, with occasional green splashed glazing, strap handles and thumbed bungs. The pale grey-white slip on the orange surfaces is the greatest marker to Bourne products at this period, though not all have it.

Other types are less certain in their origin, similar shelly, oolitic and sandy fabrics deriving from a variety of industries around Peterborough which were prolific in the same period and exploited very similar petrological sources, such as Glapthorn, near Oundle, where later 15th-century kilns have been excavated and published at Leacroft and Gypsy Lane (Johnson 1997, 13-42). It is not dissimilar in range or indeed fabric-colour from the Bourne products but the fabric is overall much harder and feels slightly 'pimply' when compared with the smooth Bourne finish. It often is slipped in the manner of Bourne, although not as extensively.

There is a noticeable absence of types from the east and south-easterly direction of Peterborough. For instance there is no Cambridge Sgraffito Ware. This is a broad observation already noted at The Still, and a pattern is emerging of a Peterborough which, in ceramic terms at least, looked to successful local industries to the west and north in the period, with little more than the ubiquitous Glazed Red earthenwares, type fossils for the later 16th century, coming from, possibly, a wide variety of sources across East Anglia, emulating Dutch imports.

Dating and context

The majority of well-stratified material is almost certainly of the 16th-17th centuries, most probably *c.*1525-1600, characterised by the regular appearance of Bourne Type D-ware in conjunction with either Cistercian ware or Midland Black, with occasional Rhenish Stoneware flagons and mugs, or sometimes a combination. Localised concentrations of Glazed Red Earthenwares are also noticeable alongside these. This is most noticeable as the consistent dating time and again for the distinctive black silty deposit which was encountered all over the site. This appears to be the flattened, strewn remains of a widespread rubbish deposit which may have formed what

Code	Description	Sherds	Weight (g)	Date
A	Thetford-type ware	1	19	12th-13th centuries
B	Grimston-type ware	7	51	13th century
C	Lyveden/Stanion A ware	5	56	c1100-1300
D	Lyveden Stanion B ware	10	178	c1250-1500
E	Bourne B ware	7	101	c1200-1500
F	Sandy Shelly ware	16	332	c1200-1500
G	Oolitic shelly ware	6	217	c1200-1500
H	Late medieval reduced ware	6	78	c1400-1500
I	Tudor Green type ware	15	30	c1400-1450
J	Glapthorn Ware	16	169	c1450-1500
K	Bourne D Ware & variants	817	15671	c1450-1637
L1	Raeren Stoneware	13	103	c1475-1550
L2	Langerwehe Stoneware	3	12	c1475-1550
L3	Frechen Stoneware	6	32	c1600-1700
M	Cistercian ware	107	607	c1480-1580
N	Midland Black ware	93	1018	c1580-1700
O	Manganese-mottled ware	12	282	c1680-1740
P	Dutch Fine Redwares	4	14	c1550-1600
Q	Glazed Red Earthenwares	139	2563	c1550-1700
R	Midland Yellow ware	39	470	c1550-1700
S	Tin Glazed earthenwares	7	80	c1650-1740
T	Slipwares	13	371	c1650-1740
U	Brown Stoneware	1	7	c1680-1750
V	Westerwald Stoneware	3	29	c1665-1800
W	Nottingham Stoneware	11	55	1700-1800
X	White salt Glazed Stoneware	21	58	c1720-1770
Y	Creamware	102	352	c1720-1780
Z	Pearlwares	2	5	c1780-1820
#	Industrially-produced wares	72	1060	19th century
Totals		1553	24020	

TABLE 4.1: POTTERY FABRICS

was widely known in the 16th century as a 'muckhill' and which characterised even the most prominent parts of many towns in the immediate post-Dissolution period. Two are known in Peterborough documents: at *Combergate End* and at *Neveles Place* next to Cowgate (Mellows 1947, 76-7). Such well-documented, and in some cases mapped, examples can be similarly found in Northampton, *Rowkes Muckhill* near the Market Square, and Coventry, *Graffery* [Greyfriars] *Muckhill* outside one of the principal city gates. They would have been neither pleasant nor aesthetic but seem to have been a result of a widespread breakdown of civic and other rubbish disposal initiatives both before and after the Dissolution of the monasteries. These initiatives do seem to have worked for a little while, in that, in many urban contexts the incidence of disposal through pit-digging on a plot-by-plot basis drops dramatically in the later 15th century, suggesting rubbish-removal, but the appearance of the muck-hills merely points to the fact that, as centralised dumps increased in size, the wider dispersal of the rubbish clearly became problematic, and with few people willing to take responsibility for their fellow citizens. In some places, such as Coventry, for instance, the activity of *The Leet*, enacting the byelaws of the local Corporation, was dominated by an ongoing battle to keep public places and features of public benefit, such as defensive ditches and mill-races, and even Dissolution sites, such as the former Cathedral-priory, clear of growing dumps of both private and trade-refuse (Dormer-Harris 1907-13; Rylatt and Mason 2003, 28, 58; Soden 2005/2013, 36-8).

Peterborough was no exception, and in relation to the marketplace byelaws are a regular occurrence in the 1540s, with regulations being noted (if not enforced) in respect of timber left lying about in the streets, dung dumped, pigs allowed to run free and drains clogged (Mellows 1947, 60-61).

At Peterborough, the marketplace in the middle of the 16th century seems also to have been an unruly place, characterised by violence and affray, and even gambling, of which some quite serious incidents are recorded around the time of The Dissolution (ibid, 58-9). It is an environment in which the smashing of ceramics, whether in use or on sale, was probably all too common.

There was certainly enough to argue about. Amidst this noisome clutter, were two out of five butchers selling rotten and even fly-blown meat and one of the two fishmongers selling less than properly prepared fish (Mellows 1947, ibid 59). There were also stalls of bread-sellers, if not necessarily bakers (ibid 65), although none of them was apparently the subject of litigation. One commodity which was banned from sale was candles –presumably it impinged upon a church monopoly (op cit 61). While the market place or *marketstede* was surrounded by tenements (tenementa), including inns such as the Black Swan and Saracen's Head, it also supported shops (shopae) and, under the hall (*aula*) of the Moot Hall, stalls (opellae) (Mellows 1947, 71-2, 83). Such stalls may have been temporary, easily disassembled or more permanent. Such structures may have accounted for the timber left lying about in the streets which the authorities spoke out against.

Questions of responsibility for cleanliness and a need for enforcement may not always have been to the fore, since Peterborough Abbey from earlier times jealously guarded its market rights in the town and was quite prepared to go to law to defend them if it felt they were being challenged (Raban 2001, docs 173, 176). However, with the Dissolution of the Abbey and its re-founding as a Cathedral, many of the old responsibilities and concerns may well have been overlooked or left unenforced in the brave new world of a post-Dissolution hierarchy. It should be no surprise to find that here in the apparently prestigious centre of Peterborough, such a pattern of refuse dumping seen in other urban centres drastically affected by late medieval urban decline and the Dissolution, is all too clear. The downward slide may have begun much earlier as it is notable that during an Episcopal Visitation in 1518, there was little to commend just about anything in the Abbey's handling of its affairs, with a general state of disrepair and an air of careless abandon prevailing around its precincts (Mellows 1947, xi-xiii).

Against this background of chaos and decay, it is perhaps not surprising to be confronted with a mélange of poorly-stratified pottery scatters and un-sealed dumps which cannot be related to any one place, frontage or plot. This is particularly so when one considers that the majority of the material derives from the nadir of the period of lowest cleanliness standards (and ironically highest documentation).

The collapse of the Bourne ceramic industry after a disastrous potting-related fire in 1637 is a useful calendar break to mark in the recording of presence/absence of the predominant Bourne D-type ware in the archaeological record at Cathedral Square. It is therefore likely that any context which was dominated by this pottery, often helpfully accompanied by Glazed Red Earthenwares, elsewhere even on its own a type fossil for the 16th-17th centuries, is almost certain to be pre-1637 in origin. The upheavals of the English Civil War (1642-9) only add to this short period in Peterborough's urban experience being seen in every way as a social watershed. One perhaps may see the ceramic break as symptomatic of a change in supply, but in actual fact, the dumping of ceramics is never again so great in the market-place, suggesting that old lax ways were tightened up or that the area began to be put to different or better-regulated use.

Key structures and deposits:

While the pottery was originally looked at following the end of the excavations, some of it has since been revisited in the light of the stratigraphic research which has accompanied the post-excavation programme.

Cathedral Square, Building 3

Pottery from the foundations and other key initial contexts relating to its construction show that Building 3, situated in the south-east corner of Cathedral Square, was built no earlier than around 1550, (Lyveden/Stanion B ware, Bourne D, Glazed Red Earthenware, Cistercian ware, Tudor Green-type ware, Midland Black ware, ?Siegburg and Frechen stoneware).

There were a number of rooms identified within it, the pottery from four of which shows it had a working life which attracted only a few sherds of the dominant Bourne D material, in no distinctive forms. Although some of the material is probably residual or intrusive during later groundworks, it is tempting to see the room as going out of use before 1637. Certainly there is no pottery within which was produced after that date. It remains possible, of course that the room uses were changed, which excluded pottery use at or before that date.

That a context may be related to the building demolition is perhaps not as helpful as may initially be surmised. This material comprises Bourne D and Glazed red earthenware again; they are ubiquitous as residual material thereafter, and the loose stratification which accompanies demolition makes them unreliable as any more than very general date indicators on their own.

In summary Building 3 is, on ceramic grounds, of unclear function, but stood in use perhaps from *c.*1550–*c.*1650.

The dark silts

These silts are presumed to be the remnants of the noisome morass of dung, against which the authorities railed and legislated. There is nothing in the ceramic to suggest otherwise, although it is suggested that they had been accumulating for some time before the documented fruitless attempts to clear them through personal fines.

Although the material within them dates over a long period, with residual material from as far back as the 12th-13th centuries included, it is again pottery of the 16th-17th centuries which predominates, suggesting the nearby buildings functioned quite acceptably adjacent to their own rubbish dumps. Once again there is a preponderance of Bourne D wares, mainly jugs, bowls and cisterns, but accompanied by a wider range of other types, albeit very fragmentary: Cistercian ware drinking cups, Midland Blackware tygs (upright tankards), Glazed Red Earthenware (probable) Tripod Pipkins (saucepans), German stoneware flagons, an unglazed lid.

One specialist type which is present appears to be a flanged bowl which may be a type of cucurbit, the bowl for collecting residues or salts, which were a by-product of both alchemy and many distilling processes. A few fragments of Tin Glazed Earthenware (undecorated) might be associated with a druggist or apothecary, since they favoured the type for its clear white glazes. It might be argued that together they may be suggestive of some chemical preparation going on nearby.

Also notable, but not for their use, are decorative fragments of German stoneware drinking flagons or biconical jugs, in particular two Westerwald-types. Although the area of the Westerwald, and particularly around the German town of Hohr-Grenzhausen, still produces cobalt-blue decorated salt-glazed wares even today, the use as here of a mix of cobalt blue and a less pure purple together, is a characteristic which commenced in 1665 (Hurst *et al* 1986, 222). This later 17th-century continuation of dumping is confirmed by a few sherds of slipware. An even later type is represented by a single sherd of Nottingham stoneware, no earlier than *c.*1700.

It seems therefore that the dumping which may have begun at the turn of the 15th to the 16th centuries, and reached its height in the well documented local legislation of *c.*1550 continued, potentially unabated, through the period of Bourne D dominance which ended in 1637, and then on past 1665 and the remainder of the 17th century.

The local experience of Peterborough marketplace was one of an apparent messy potential health-hazard, which persisted regardless of monastic, cathedral or civic oversight for over 200 years.

Building stone
by Jackie Hall

One stone vessel (a mortar), ten architectural fragments and numerous stone slate and geological samples were retrieved and submitted for analysis. The vessel and architectural fragments are medieval, while the geological samples and Collyweston roof slates may be either medieval or post-medieval. Although all the fragments are, inevitably, found in secondary contexts (re-use or destruction), they are all stratified. They have a part to play in our understanding of the development of the city, particularly the rebuilding of the parish church in the market place and the concomitant demolition of both the original parish church on the east side of the abbey and the nave of the chapel of St Thomas Becket next to the great gateway into the abbey.

Stone mortar

The single stone mortar is of an ornate type usually dated to the late 13th or 14th centuries (along with many other types), but it was found reused in a potentially much later context (Figs 3.21, 3.22). With such long-lived material, residuality is commonplace, as demonstrated, for instance, by the chronological distribution of mortars from Winchester (Biddle and Smith 1990, 891). This example, however, is unusual in being actively reused despite the hole in its base – or, perhaps, because of it, probably many years after its manufacture.

It is made of oolitic fossiliferous stone, probably Barnack, although another source cannot be ruled out. About 60% survives in three large and three small fragments, with half to nearly full height and two ribs/lugs (Fig 4.1). The mortar stands on a square base, whose angles are created by broad ribs that widen and join at the base. Above one of the surviving ribs is a rectangular lug and on the other is a triangular panel, almost certainly indicative of a runnel (for a spout) that has worn away. The interior is smooth (diameter 280mm), and the whole is worn and damaged, with a large irregular hole in the base, possibly the result of pounding, although the narrowing of the wall at the top of the sloping base might rather suggest grinding (Dunning 1977, 321).

It is similar to some mortars imported from Normandy (eg Caen types 1 and 6; Dunning 1977, 334-6 and 341-2), as well as to examples from the south and east of England made from a variety of different stone types (eg Salisbury no. 9; Drinkwater 1991, 170 and Winchester 3167; Biddle and Smith 1990, 902-3; Saffron Waldon and Boston; Dunning 1961, 281-2). Late 13th/14th century, (1762), SF79.

Architectural stone in Alwalton marble

Alwalton marble, quarried from the banks of the River Nene only four miles from the centre of Peterborough, was a high status building material, used in the same way as Purbeck marble to architecturally enrich a building (Blair 1991; Alexander 1995, 118-22). It was used at Peterborough in the first quarter of the 13th century on the west front of the abbey church (now the cathedral), where it can still be seen in profusion, but it is barely represented in the local parish churches. It was, however, used in other high status buildings such as Lincoln Minster, Ely Cathedral, Bury St Edmund's abbey and Thetford Abbey (ibid and Hall 2004).

Thus, the presence of two pieces of Alwalton in the Cathedral Square excavations is of considerable interest, and they could have got there in two different ways. Most recently, in 1650, after the depredations of the Civil War, many buildings of the former abbey were taken down and sold, including the chapter house, the library, infirmary, cloisters, Lady Chapel and a number of houses (Hall 2014). This origin within the abbey would reinforce the elite status of Alwalton marble, and the style of the capital fits with the documentary date of the Lady Chapel. However, the street monument almost certainly predates 1650 (certainly, if it is the one shown on Speed's map of 1610).

More likely, then, the capital originated in one of the buildings taken down to provide building material for the new church of St John the Baptist in 1402 namely either the old parish church or the nave of the chapel of St Thomas Becket. The capital is of a suitable size for a modest parish church or aisled chapel and its presence in either of these buildings would indicate significant investment by the abbey in a church/ chapel for local lay use.

Capital

Part of a splendid octagonal/semi-octagonal polished Alwalton marble capital, even though the top, bottom and rear are broken (Fig 4.2). What remains of the moulding – from the bottom: a hollow, fillet, half-roll, small angled fillet, and beginning of another moulding (probably a scroll) above. The octagonal shaft below would be no more than 230mm across. Late 13th to mid-14th centuries, SF58, base of street monument (1174).

Shaft

Fragment of Alwalton marble shaft, diameter 99mm, surviving length 129mm (top and bottom do not survive); part of surface blackened by burning; otherwise surface in very good condition as if not exposed for very long, 13th century. From 17th/18th-century robber trench (1148), Building 3. Not illustrated.

Other architectural stone from the Street Monument

As well as the Alwalton marble capital (above), six further stones were retrieved from the base of the street monument. They are all of Barnack stone, three of them plain ashlar or unworked. The remaining three (below) are not very diagnostic of date but, like the capital, probably also originate in the old church of St John the Baptist or the nave of the chapel of St Thomas Becket, prior to their reuse.

Fragment of Barnack slab, 72mm thick, with a small part of one rounded edge surviving. The top is worn suggesting it may have been a step prior to its re-use. (1174), SF56. Not illustrated.

Possible step, or part of late medieval ground-course, height 198mm, with a projecting half-roll at the top of 85mm diameter (Fig 4.3). With fine vertical tooling on front, rough diagonal tooling on one side. The stone is cut from Barnack and is not worn, suggesting a short period of use prior to its re-use in Cathedral Square, (1174), SF59.

A finely cut stone, with one 90° angle and one 135° angle; faint vertical tooling on two faces and fine diagonal on one face, probably part of a respond/jamb, (1174), SF60 (Fig 4.4).

Other architectural stone

Only two other stones are worth noting, one with an octagonal moulding and one with cut off iron bars.

Possible corbel; part-octagonal, 186-192mm high, with a half-roll at the top 82mm diameter with a long receding chamfer below. The (originally) visible faces are worn, but diagonal tooling is faintly visible on the end beds. Probably 13th century, dark silt (1112) 16th/17th century (Fig 4.5).

A lump of very shelly Barnack; extremely worn before its re-use, but with the possible remains of two or three worked faces. On one side is a lump of iron fixed with lead. It may possibly have held two projecting railings. SF77, dark silt (1214), 16th-17th centuries. Not illustrated.

Catalogue of worked stone illustrations

(Figs 4.1-4.5)

1 A medieval mortar in Barnack limestone (SF79)
2 Octagonal capital or base in Alwalton marble (SF58)
3 Possible step, with a half-roll (SF59)
4 Part of respond/jamb (SF60)
5 Part of an octagonal moulding, possibly a corbel

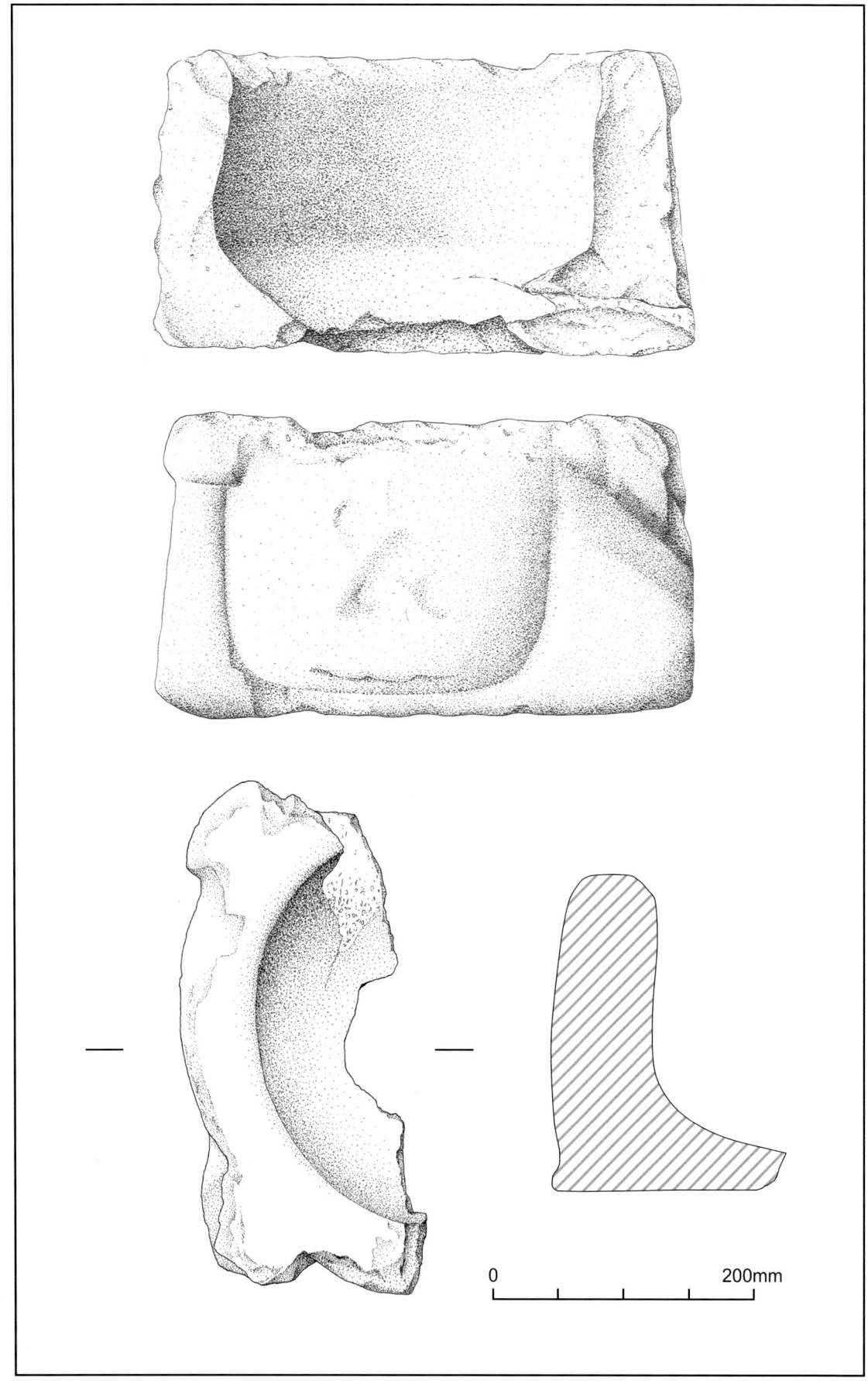

Fig 4.1: Medieval mortar in Barnack limestone (SF79)

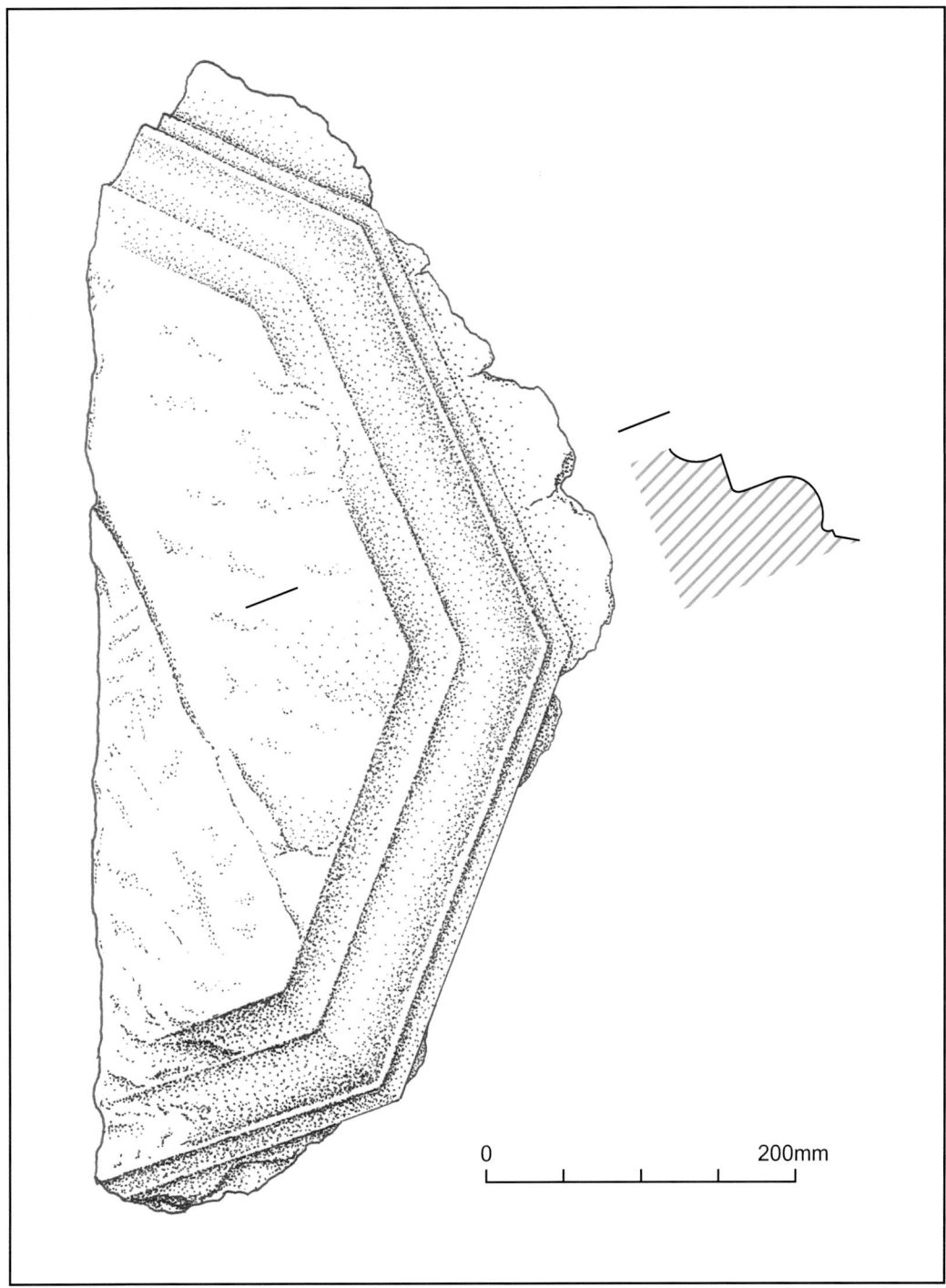

Fig 4.2: Octagonal capital or base in Alwalton marble (SF58)

Stone roof tile
by Pat Chapman and Jackie Hall

The 22 roof tiles range from almost complete tiles to small fragments. There is a wide variety of colours, from buff to dark grey, and also quite a wide range of thicknesses *c.*7mm-30mm, but nonetheless all the fragments of stone roof slate are of Collyweston, a distinctively sandy limestone. For full description see Sutherland (2003, 72-4).

There are three rectangular or tapering rectangular tiles, 325-190mm long by 185-160mm wide, each with a round peghole. Two tiles are bell-shaped, that is triangular with a rounded top. One is 250mm high, tapering from 130 at the top to 280mm at the base, and the second one is 200mm high and tapers from 40-150mm.

These roof tiles are medieval to early post-medieval in date, the same as the ceramic roof tiles. There are no Welsh slates to indicate a mid-19th century or later date.

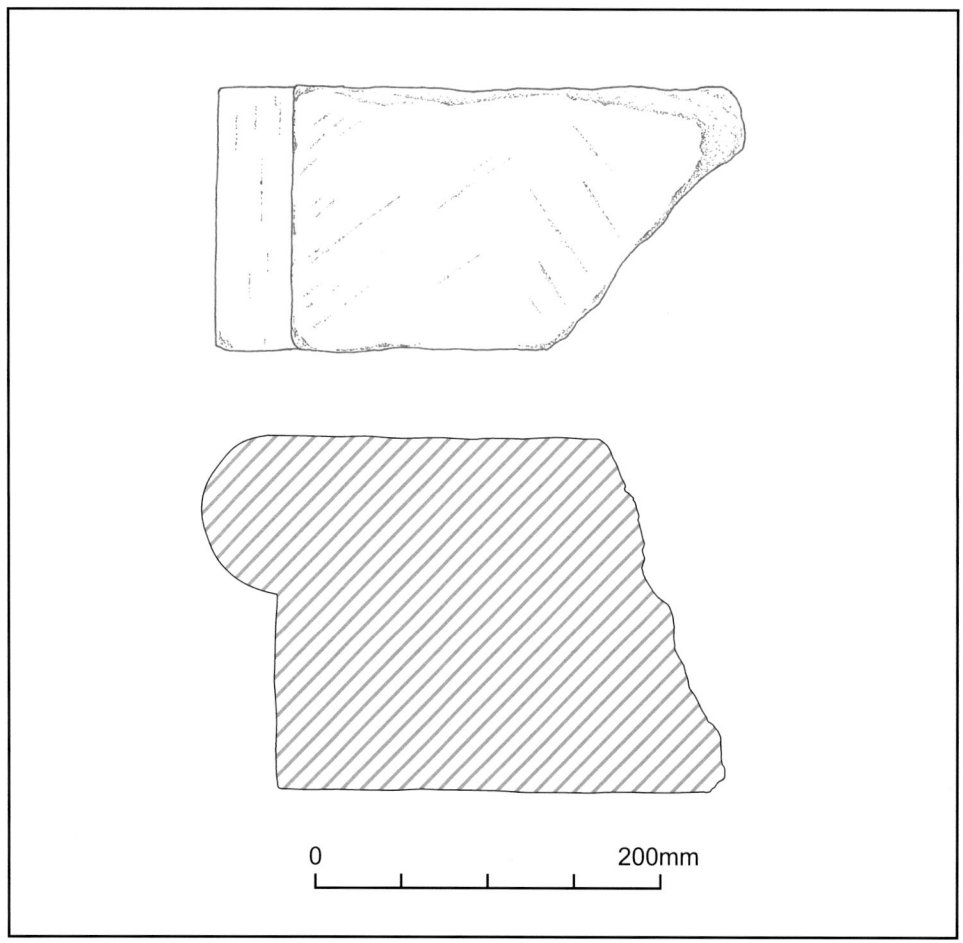

Fig 4.3: Possible corbel, with a half roll

Other finds
by Tora Hylton, with Andy Chapman and Ian Meadows

The excavations produced a collection of finds spanning the late medieval and post-medieval periods. Successive episodes of reorganisation, together with the remains of a widespread silt deposit had produced a predominantly residual assemblage. No finds were recovered from deposits predating the c.15th century. The majority of finds were recovered from a fine black silty organic deposit which extended over much of the medieval cobbled surface of the market square. Small numbers of finds were also recovered from floors surviving within buildings and on pitched-stone surfaces. In tandem with other urban sites, this assemblage encompasses a range of costume fittings, domestic equipment and tools which presumably had been casually lost or discarded along with the household waste and general rubbish from the market.

There are 193 individual or group recorded small finds, providing a total number of c.263 individual objects in five material types (Table 4.2). Each object has been described and measured and a descriptive catalogue is retained in the archive.

Material	Total
Copper alloy (excluding coins)	56
Iron objects	64
Lead	38
Bone	1
Glass	35
Total	193

Table 4.2: Other finds quantified by material type

Fifteen objects were submitted for X-ray. This was undertaken by Wiltshire Conservation Service. This not only provided a permanent record, but it enabled identification and revealed technical details not previously visible. There is a knife handle decorated with non-ferrous tubular rivets and pins and three copper alloy objects have been preserved by the anaerobic conditions and so still retain their original 'bright' surfaces.

The finds

No finds were recovered from features predating the 15th century, although some residual finds may originate from

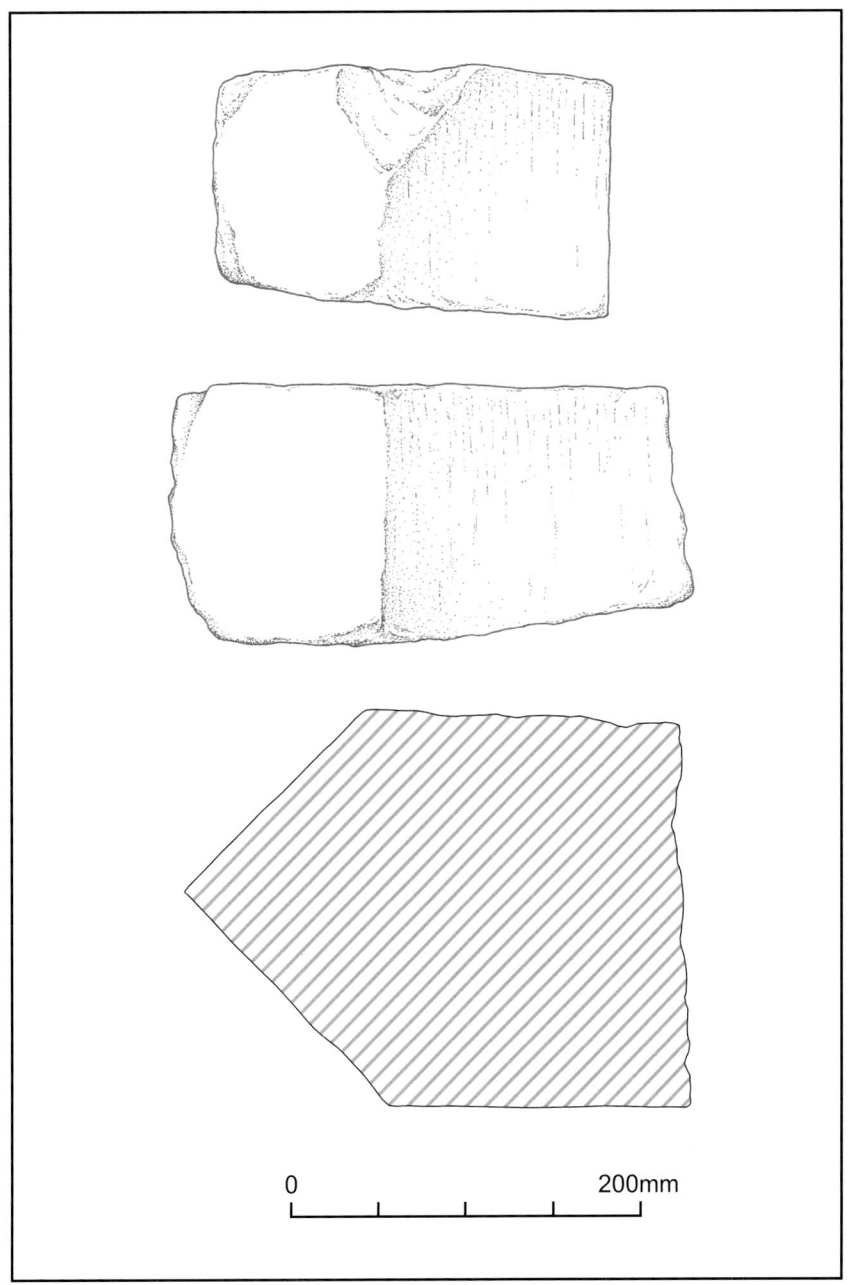

FIG 4.4: PART OF RESPOND/JAMB (SF60)

earlier phases of occupation. For example a buzz bone, presumably predating the 15th century, was recovered from 16th-century silt deposits [1016].

The largest number of individually/group recorded small finds, c. 190, were recovered from a fine black silty organic deposit which extended over much of the medieval cobbled surface of the market square. This silty deposit derived from the waste discarded from the tenements and markets in the late medieval and post-medieval period. It contained a large amount of preserved leather (see below), iron nails and undiagnostic fragments. However, there is a small group of identifiable artefacts which can be assigned specific uses; these are dominated by dress accessories and items for domestic use (Table 4.3).

Dress accessories are represented by small portable items which would have formed part of a person's attire. There are buckles for securing shoe straps and belts, SF85 (1417), (Fig 4.6, 6); a mount for enhancing items of leather or textile, SF75 (1661), (Fig 4.6, 7), and lace chapes and pins for securing items of clothing. In addition, there is a cast strap fitting with suspension hook, SF12, (05/6), (Fig 4.6, 8) and part of a purse frame with niello decoration, SF64 (1186), (Fig 4.6, 9).

Finds for domestic use are represented by a cast tripod cauldron, SF5 (05/15), (Fig 4.6, 10); part of a skimmer for removing fats etc. from food; a candle holder, SF62 (1186), (Fig 4.6, 11), and a key for a mounted lock, SF50 (1186),

FIG 4.5: PART OF AN OCTAGONAL MOULDING, POSSIBLY A STEP (SF59)

(Fig 4.6, 12). With the exception of nails there is a dearth of general building equipment, the only identifiable item is a single hinge pivot for fixing a window/shutter.

Other finds include a rowle from a spur, SF47 (1186), (Fig 4.6, 15) and three thimbles; two illustrated, SF71 (1125) and SF66 (1186), (Fig 4.6,13 and 14).

Other notable concentrations include an assemblage of finds recovered from a floor within the late c.15th-17th century building, Building 3, in the south-east corner of Cathedral Square. The finds include part of a pair of shears, and a cloth seal, SF10 (1078), (Fig 4.6, 16), which together may allude to the building's use. In addition, there was a lace chape, a purse frame and a large deposit of window glass, some 576 shards, recovered together with fragments of decaying H-sectioned lead window cames.

Three pieces of lead shot were recovered from a pitched-stone surface.

Personal possessions

This category comprises small portable items which would have formed part of a person's clothing (costume fittings), or held by an individual for personal use (recreation).

Functional category	Quantity
Personal Possessions	
Costume and jewellery	24
Personal equipment	2
Building equipment	
General ironwork	1
Nails	104
Window glass	c 600 fragments
Window lead	9
Household equipment	5
Vessel glass	c 20 fragments
Knives	3
Horse Equipment	1
Trade	1
Tools: textile working	4
Weapons (lead shot)	3
Miscellaneous and unidentified	
Copper alloy	26
Iron	18
Lead	20

TABLE 4.3: OTHER FINDS BY FUNCTIONAL CATEGORY

Buckles

There are four buckles. Three small lead alloy buckles, SF48 and SF112 (1186) and SF113 (1222), for use with shoes were recovered from silt deposits dating to the 16th century. The frames are circular with a circular cross-section and they measure *c.*12-15mm in diameter. Two of the frames still retain iron wire pins which have been folded around the frame. Typologically they represent early/mid-15th-century forms (cf Grew and de Neergaard 1988, fig 110, b). An iron buckle attached to the remains of a heavy duty leather strap, SF85 (1417), was recovered from 18th-century silt deposits. The buckle is covered in corrosion products, but the X-ray reveals a rectangular frame, *c.*34mm x 30mm, with a circular cross-section and a sheet cylinder around the outside edge (Fig 4.6, 6). The leather strap is folded around the inside edge of frame and secured by six rivets (four extant). Buckles of this type would have been hard wearing and the sheet cylinder would have ensured tighter fastening. They could have had any number of uses from securing belts to harness straps (cf Margeson 1993, fig 18, 197).

A copper alloy buckle-plate, SF2 (1013), was recovered from 16th-century silt. It is a one-piece type that has been manufactured from a rectangular sheet of copper alloy folded widthways, 32mm x 21mm. There are two opposing cut-outs for the frame and two centrally-placed, close-set perforations adjacent to the attachment edge for securing to the leather strap. The attachment edge is furnished with five alternate small/large V-shaped notches, rather like that seen on a 15th-century strap-end from London (Pritchard 1991, fig 94, 684).

Lace chapes

Six chapes for securing the ends of laces were found, each made from copper alloy sheet rolled to form a tapered tube with an edge to edge seam (cf Egan 1991, fig 182). Four of the chapes are complete and range in recorded length from 15-73mm.

There are five small tapered lace chapes, SF96, 98, 99, 118 and SF16 (1162, 1186, 1214, 1186 and 1323 respectively), complete examples measure 15-20mm long, 3mm in diameter and the terminal is open ended, they were all recovered from the silt [1162, 1186, 1214, 1323]. One large chape, SF27, was found on the floor of room 11, Building 3 [1078]; it is 73mm long and 5mm-8mm in diameter, like an example from London the terminal is sealed with a folded tab (Egan 1991, fig 188, 1441).

Mounts

A single repoussé belt mount with central and terminal lobes, SF75, is from the churchyard pitched-stone surface (1661) (Fig 4.6, 7). The terminal lobes have a perforated boss with a cable border and the central boss is perforated. Similar examples are known from Norwich (Margeson 1993, fig 23, 276) and York (Ottaway and Rogers 2002, fig 1479, 13369). They date to *c.*1400-1600 AD.

Pins

Ten copper alloy pins and one spherical pin head in a white metal alloy, SF24 (1016), were recovered. Eight of the pins are complete and measure 28-55mm long. Four head types are represented. The earliest appear to be those with bi-conical heads, SF33 (1333), up to 55mm long; wound wire heads up to 30mm long from (1186) and one incomplete pin with a flat circular head, SF104 (1186), all these types were recovered from 16th-century deposits. Finer pins with small spherical heads, SF41 and SF68 (1125 and 1186), up to 43mm long, were recovered from later contexts. This type would have been used for sewing and for securing pleats and ruffs etc.

Miscellaneous fittings

Other fastenings/fittings related to dress include a copper alloy wire loop fastener, SF75,(1214) with the terminal ends twisted together (cf. Margeson 1993, fig 10, 98-101) and a cast copper alloy strap fitting in the form of a suspension hook, SF12 (5/6), (Fig 4.6, 8), both date to 16th/17th-centuries. The fitting comprises a small domed boss with an integral 'rectangular' plate, slightly tapered, beneath. The boss is pierced by a copper alloy rivet for attachment. Corrosion deposits obscure the presence of a further rivet in the rectangular plate. From the lower edge of the plate protrudes an integral rearward facing suspension hook (now damaged) with a D-shaped cross-section. Margeson indicates that strap fittings of this form would have been hung from a loop on a bar attached to a sword-belt, and the slings for the sword would be attached to the mount by the rivets (1993, 38).

Purse frame

There are fragments from two cast copper alloy purse frames. Both have U-shaped cross-sections and typologically represent known forms. The largest fragment is 158mm long, SF64 (1186), and was recovered from silt deposits. The inner edge of the frame is perforated for attaching to textile or leather purses and the outer edge is decorated with a deep-grooved lattice motif filled with niello and the end of the frame terminates in a short spike (swivel point) for securing the frame to the bar (Fig 4.6, 9). Purse frames of this type are not uncommon, they date to the 16th and 17th centuries and similar examples are known from Winchester (Biddle 1990, fig 142, 1347) and Norwich (Margeson 1993, fig 24, 290).

The other purse frame was from the floor of Building 3, SF25 (1094). It survives to 78mm long, the frame is plain and the X-ray reveals that it has two small circular perforations, 45mm apart, along the inner edge (cf Ward Perkins, 1993, plate XXXV).

Recreation

A single buzz-bone manufactured from a pig metapodia, SF87 (1016), was recovered from silt deposits. It is 73mm long and has perforations, 4-5mm in diameter, laterally through the anterior and posterior surfaces. The terminals do not appear to have been modified although there is some damage at one end. These objects are common finds in Britain and on the continent on sites of Saxon and medieval date and although there is some dispute as to their function (cf MacGregor *et al* 1999, 1980-81), these days it is generally assumed that they would have been mounted on a twisted string and used as a buzzing, spinning toy. Since an example from Beverley was found to be threaded with a knotted leather thong (Foremen 1992, fig 84, 505), this interpretation has gained support.

Building equipment

There are very few finds which relate to the structures that may have existed. With the exception of nails and a hinge pivot for hanging a door/shutter, there is a dearth of items relating to internal fixtures and fittings. The hinge pivot, SF50 (1434), was recovered from silt. It comprises a circular-sectioned pivot (guide arm) and tapered, rectangular-sectioned shank, 84mm long. The shank would have been driven into wood, leaving the pivot, 35mm long but incomplete, free to retain the hanging eye of a strap hinge attached to a door/shutter.

The greatest concentration of building debris was recovered from a floor [1066] of the 16th century in Building 3. In total, *c*.576 shards of glass were recovered, together with fragments of decayed plain (unmilled) H-sectioned lead cames up to 75mm long and a possible setting bar. The range of shards suggests that this assemblage may be a waste deposit of crown glass. It contains 170 unusable fragments with curved edges, 20% by number, and *c*.392 miscellaneous fragments with no distinguishing features, 68%. There are no complete quarries and just 14 shards, 3%, preserve vestiges of a single grozed edge. If this deposit was the remains of a window, evidence for complete or partially complete quarry fragments would be expected, or at the very least the percentage of fragments with grozed edges should be higher.

Part of a possible setting bar was also recovered. Setting bars are used for securing metal bars into prepared holes in masonry; the melted lead would have been poured around the end of the bar to form a fixing (Egan 2005, 348, 99). The recess/void within the lead indicates that the bar was parallel-sided, 125mm long and 20mm wide. The terminal of the void is stepped.

Household equipment

There are a small number of fragmentary items for use within a domestic setting. These include objects relating to the preparation of food, security and lighting. All were recovered from 16th-century silt contexts.

Kitchen ware

There is a rim fragment from a cast copper alloy tripod cauldron, SF5 (05/15) (Fig 4.6,10). The rim is out-turned and measurements suggest that if complete it would have measured *c*.380mm in diameter. Attached to the outside of the rim is part of a C-shaped lug to which a handle would have been attached. The form displays similarities to an example from London which was recovered from a 14th/15th-century deposit (Egan 1998, fig 131, 446).

Six fragments from a crudely perforated copper alloy disc, *c*.40mm in diameter, appear to be part of a skimmer, SF102 (1214), a utensil for skimming fat, cream or foods. Similar examples are known from Luggershall Castle (Robinson and Griffiths 2000, fig 6.12, 112) and London (Egan 1998, fig 126).

Finally there is a copper alloy rim fragment from a flatware vessel measuring *c*.180-190mm in diameter, SF3 (1006).

Key

The key is for use with a mounted lock and is a type which could be used from both sides, SF50 (1186). It has a D-shaped bow, solid tapered stem with stopped over bit (Fig 4.6,12). The stem does not project beyond the symmetrical bit, which has simple wards running horizontally. Keys of this type were in use from the late medieval into the post-medieval period.

Candle holder

A single iron cup from a candle holder, SF62 (1186), is outward facing, 15mm in diameter and 25mm high (Fig 4.6, 11). A vertical spike/arm, in line with the side of the cup protrudes from the lower edge and the broken terminal bends out at right angles. It is difficult to be sure which type of candle holder this originates from. It may be part of a candle holder and rushlight as illustrated by Egan (1998, fig 113, 420) or a cupped candle holder with a driptray (ibid 1998, fig 110, 410).

Vessel glass

Over 20 fragments of vessel glass were recovered from deposits dating from the 16th to the 19th centuries. The majority are undiagnostic body sherds. With the exception of a base sherd from a small bottle/flask in pale blue glass from silt deposits, all the vessel fragments were recovered from 18th and 19th-century contexts. Diagnostic forms include fragments of 18th-century wine bottles, small flasks/bottles and a faceted stem from a wine goblet in clear glass.

Tools

There is a small collection of tools, they include part of a pair of shears and three thimbles from 16th-century silt deposits, these presumably used for activities relating to wool/textile working and three knives from 16th to 18th-century deposits.

Shears

Part of a bow and arm from a pair of shears, SF16 (1078), was recovered from the floor of 16th-century Building 3, together with a lead cloth seal. The stem has an oval/D-shaped cross-section and tapers slightly towards blade. The stem expands to form rectangular sectioned bow, however, the bow does not flair like later examples suggesting an early date.

Thimbles

Three complete thimbles were recovered from 16th-century silt deposits. All are cast with hand punched indentations. There are two small thimbles, 15-19mm in diameter, and 15mm high, SF71 and SF3, both from (1125). They have small indentations for narrow gauge needles and their size suggests that they would have been used for light duties, finer work and lighter fabrics. One, SF71, has a small perforation at the centre of the tonsure (Fig 4.6, 13). Finally, there is one heavy duty thimble, SF66 (1186), 20mm in diameter and 24mm high. It has large indentations placed in concentric circles and presumably would have been used for coarse cloth or leather (Fig 4.6, 14).

Knives

There are three single-edged blades and all were recovered from stratified deposits. They have been classified according to the method of attaching the handle. There are two whittle tang knives and one scale tang knife. The former terminate in a tapered prong, on to which a handle of wood, bone or horn would have been hafted and the latter terminate with an integral, parallel-sided perforated strip, to which scales of wood or bone were riveted.

Whittle-tang knives

There are two incomplete whittle–tang knives. The most complete example, SF18, *c*.93mm, was recovered from a 17th-century makeup layer (807) and typologically it is post-medieval in date. The tang is in line with the back of the blade and at the junction there is a long bolster measuring 50mm long. The cutting edge is horizontal. The second knife, SF42 (1417), comprises just a rectangular-sectioned tang with a vestige of blade, recovered from an 18th-century silt layer associated with the Corn Exchange.

Scale-tang knife

Part of a knife handle/tang from a scale-tang knife, SF39 (1028), was recovered from a 16th-century soil mound. Just a small fragment of the tang, 53x11mm, survives, together with the remains of mineral preserved wood adhering to the surface of the strip. The X-ray reveals that the wood is held in place by three non-ferrous tubular rivets and that it is decorated with copper alloy rivets and pins forming a trefoil motif. The form of decoration is similar to that seen on an example from Norwich (Margeson 1993, fig 95, 864).

Trade

The only item related to trade is a cloth seal, SF105 (1078), which was recovered from the floor of 16th-century Building 3. It comprises two flat discs, 20mm in diameter, one with an integral rivet connected by a rectangular strip (Fig 4.6, 16). The discs would have been folded around the edge of the fabric, so that the rivet was pushed through the fabric and into the hole of the second disc. It would have then been stamped with the cloth/merchants mark (Egan 1985). This seal is marked with initials, one legible 'M' in Lombardic script and the other illegible. The presence of initials suggests that it is probably a clothier's or weavers seal.

Horse equipment

Horse equipment is represented by a worn and partially incomplete star rowle, SF47 (1186), of six oval-sectioned points (one missing and three incomplete) (Fig 4.6, 15). The rowle measures 52mm in diameter, typologically rowles of this size generally date to the 15th and 16th centuries (Ellis 1993, 223, 1807).

Weapons

Three pieces of lead shot were recovered from a pitched-stone surface [1075]. Two are 13mm in diameter, SF32 and SF33 (1075), and one, a small spherical lead pellet is 7mm in diameter, SF35 (1075). Their size suggests that they would have been for use with a pistol. Two have possible impact marks indicating that they have either been used or dropped.

Catalogue of Illustrated finds

(Fig 4.6, 6-16)

6   Iron buckle attached to leather strap, secured by six rivets (four extant), 34x30mm, strap length 50mm, SF85, (1417) dark silt, Corn Exchange, 18th century
7   Copper alloy repoussé mount with terminal and central lobes, 15x32mm, SF75, (1661) buried soil/silt, late17th/18th centuries
8   Copper alloy strap fitting with suspension loop, 13x53mm, SF12, (5-6) stone surface, late 16th/17th centuries
9   Copper alloy purse frame with niello-ornament in the form of a lattice motif, SF64, (1186) dark silt, 16th century
10 Fragment of cast copper alloy tripod cauldron, SF5, (5-15) dark silt, 13th-16th centuries
11 Iron candle holder, internal diameter of cup 15mm, height 25mm, SF62, (1186) dark silt, 16th century
12 Iron key for mounted lock, length 92mm, SF50, (1186) dark silt, 16th century
13 Copper alloy thimble, hand-punched indentations, bare tonsure with small perforation at the centre, diameter 15mm, height 15mm, SF71, (1125) dark silt, 16th century
14 Copper alloy thimble, hand-punched indentations, diameter 20mm, height 24mm, PCSF09, SF66, (1186) dark silt, 16th century
15 Copper alloy star rowle with six oval-sectioned worn points, diameter 52mm, SF47, (1186) dark silt, 16th century
16 Lead cloth seal, circular two-disc seal type, diameter 20mm, SF105, (1078), building floor, 16th century

Millstone

by Andy Chapman

Over the remnant of Building 1, in the possible wall foundations (729/741) for Building 3, of 16th-17th century date, there were two joining fragments from the circumference of a lower millstone in Millstone Grit. The stone is 700mm in diameter, 70mm thick at the circumference and up to 95mm thick. These dimensions indicate that it has come from a water or wind-powered mill. The under surface has been worked level and this and the circumference retain closely-spaced dimpled tool marks. The convex grinding surface is worn, but not heavily, and dimpled tool marks survive particularly in a 60mm band at the circumference. The small size of the stone suggests that it has come from a medieval or early post-medieval mill.

Wood
Ian Meadows

The assemblage was dominated by undiagnostic fragments of wood, mostly showing no evidence of having been cut or worked along with many small twigs or pieces of small branches. This is perhaps to be expected from a town where the buildings were largely timber-built. The area they were recovered from was, in the medieval and post-medieval period, an open space with few permanent structures so the pieces recovered may have been derived from activity in the adjacent structures or in temporary market booths. That at least one piece shows signs of burning might reflect an *ad hoc* view to fires in the market place, although of course it could have fallen from a brazier being used to cook/keep warm. The fragments of burr wood, SF37, and the removed knot, SF92, and indeed the many twig fragments, SF92, may reflect the preparation of pieces of wood for working. The absence of wood shaving or what could be recognised as turning waste might suggest that either such activity took place elsewhere or the material was either burnt or too ephemeral to survive archaeologically.

The occurrence of several pieces of board/plank is not surprising as they could be derived from a wide variety of sources. Of interest is the possible hairpin, SF93, and possible wooden bowl fragment, SF53, both types of artefacts known elsewhere from waterlogged urban contexts. The absence of larger fragments or structural timber possibly reflects that the fragments left in the market square were small enough to not be worth picking up to use as fuel and as an assemblage it tells us little about life in Peterborough.

Coins
Ian Meadows

Eight coins were recovered. They are listed in chronological order below.

A hammered silver penny of the post-1279 long cross type. Part of the reverse mint name is visible in the legend CIVI and in the fourth quarter the legend commences with what looks like an S. The coin is probably an issue of Edward I 1272-1307, SF55 (1024)

Almost certainly a jetton on the grounds of its size, 23mm diameter. It is, however, unclear if it is one of the

3. The Archaeology of Cathedral Square

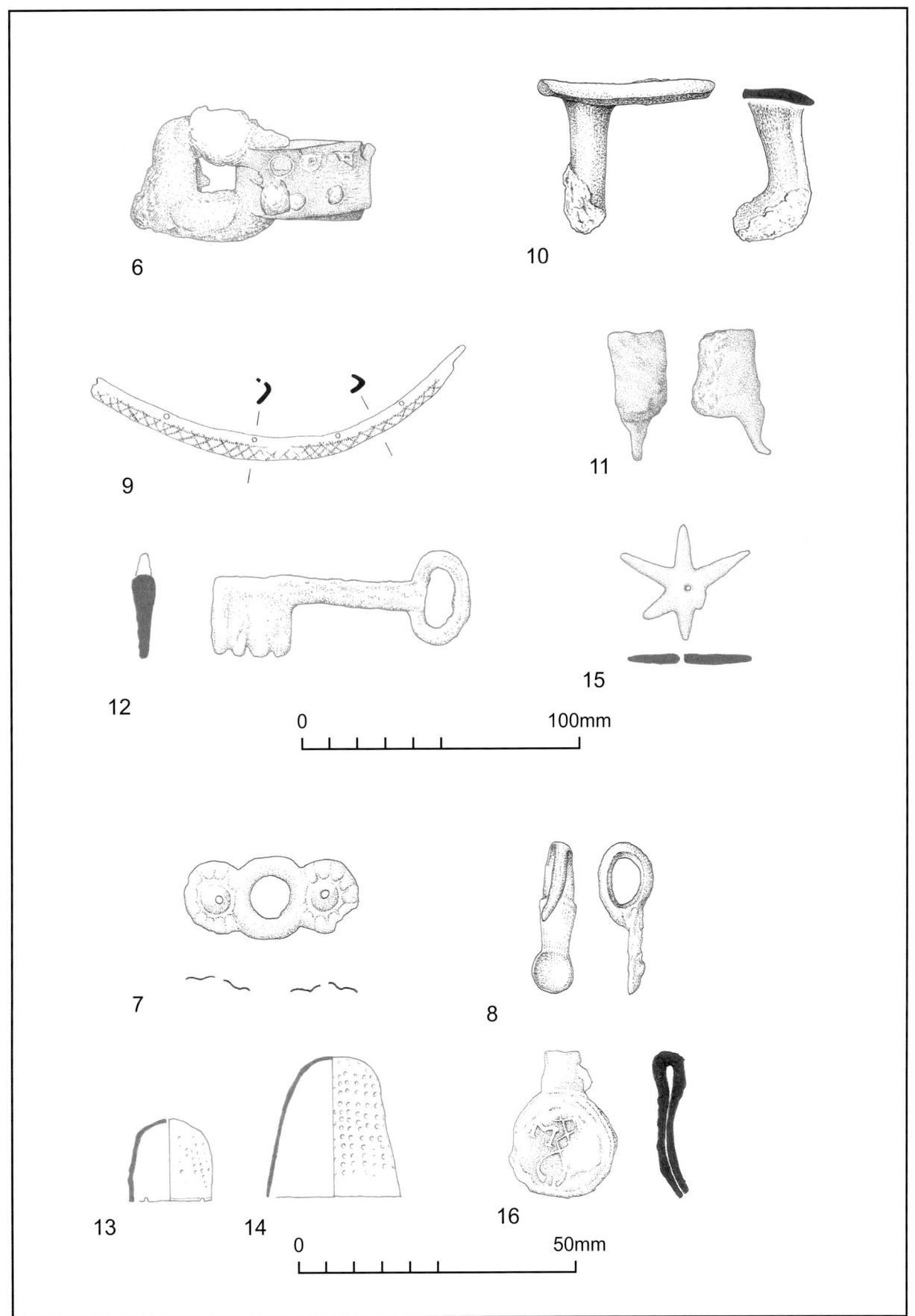

Fig 4.6: Metal finds (6-16)

English or German series. As a copper alloy flan it is too thin to be a post-medieval small denomination coin, SF38 (1147)

Probably a trade token of the 17th century, 20mm diameter, the apparent thinness of the flan would preclude an official issue coin, SF63 (1626)

Rose Farthing of Charles I, on the grounds of size, 12mm diameter, SF1 (1006)

A half penny of the period from Charles II through to George III on the grounds of the flan size, 28mm diameter), and the weight, SF66 (1646)

A late 16th or early 17th-century Nuremberg jetton, 22mm diameter. The obverse legend reads HANS SCHULTES IN NVREMBERG around three crowns, alternately with three lis, arranged around a central rose. The reverse bears an Imperial orb within a tressure of three arches and three angles with the legend GLICK KVMPT VON GOT ALEIN (good fortune comes from God alone). This piece would have served as a counting token, SF74 (1661)

If it was a coin, it would on the grounds of size be a farthing, 24mm diameter. It is unclear of which monarch and it is always possible it is a trade token of the 18th century, SF67 (1646)

Probably an 18th-century half penny, 28.5mm diameter. SF72 (1653)

With the exception of the silver Edward I penny (SF55), these flans were all copper alloy and generally highly corroded leaving no visible surface traces to use in their identification. All identifications are therefore tentative, based upon flan size and weight. The presence of possible trade tokens is noteworthy since they were recovered from the market area of the town, it is unfortunate they are not legible. The coins are likely to span the period from the Restoration to George III, but they are individually so corroded that a much closer identification is unlikely. The silver penny is also quite corroded and unfortunately even in oblique light it is not possible to discern the obverse legend.

Leather
by Quita Mould

Leather was recovered from four interventions, but principally from the watching brief. All the leather came from an extensive, fine, black, silty organic deposit that directly overlaid the medieval cobbled surface of the market square; the only exception being the remains of two shoe repair patches, SF94, recovered from a possible resurface (1187) of the Cathedral Square surface itself. Pottery found in the same dark silts dated from late medieval through to the 17th century as did the leather recovered. The shoe leather was independently datable and other leather items could be dated by close association with it; consequently the leather has been considered by date in this report where appropriate.

Methodology

The leather was wet and washed when examined and recorded. Currently it is packed wet in double, self-sealed polythene bags within a plastic storage box: it has not been conserved. A basic record of the leather in the form of an Excel Worksheet accompanies this report for inclusion in the site archive. The entries are listed by site code in context order. All measurements are in millimeter's (mm). A plus (+) indicates an incomplete measurement. Shoe sizing has been calculated according to the modern English Shoe-Size scale with the turnshoe sole and welted insole measurements rounded up to the nearest size as necessary, continental sizing is provided in brackets. No allowance has been made for shrinkage. Leather species were identified by hair follicle pattern using a low-powered magnification. Where the grain surface of the leather was heavily worn identification was not always possible. The grain pattern of sheep and goat skins are difficult to distinguish and have been grouped together as sheep/goat when the distinction could not be made. Similarly, the term bovine has been used when uncertainly arose between mature cattle hide and immature calfskin. Shoe bottom components and repairs are assumed to be of cattle hide unless stated otherwise.

The drawing conventions and terms used in the text are those commonly employed in the relevant literature and the constructions and seams are fully described elsewhere (Grew and de Neergaard 1988, 44-51; Goubitz et al 2001, 35-8; Evans and Mould 2005, 59-63). The term scrap has been used in the basic record to describe fragments of leather with all edges torn and no diagnostic features present.

Late medieval footwear

Shoe leather of late medieval date was found in five individual contexts (05-15); (1222); (1328), (1434) and (1629); all dark silt deposits of late medieval to early post-medieval date. A narrow waist area broken from a turnshoe sole, SF81, from dark silt (1222), attributed to the 16th century, was in a highly abraded condition indicating it was residual in this context. The largest group of leatherwork to be recovered from the Cathedral Square excavations came from dark silt (1434), dated to the 14th-16th centuries. The group from (1434) comprised twenty-nine turnshoe parts along with waste leather. The shoe parts present were, for the most part, heavily worn and seven had been repaired.

The group included six sole repair patches, known as clumps, including an unused example cut from a reused shoe sole, SF128 (Fig 4.7, 17), along with a seam cut away from a sole, SF56.9. Five, 17%, had secondary cutting indicating that any reusable leather had been salvaged from them for use elsewhere before they were discarded. The shoe leather from two further contexts (05-15) and [1328] was also found along with waste leather; shoe leather from the latter context having secondary cutting. This, together with the nature of the late medieval leather assemblage, suggested it to be the sweepings cleared from a cobbler's workshop or workshops (see below).

No complete or near complete turnshoes of late medieval date were present but the soles had characteristics that suggested a late 14th–15th century date, including pointed toes, long narrow waists and the occurrence of pieced soles (two-part soles). Though the turnshoe uppers were broken and incomplete three styles could be recognised: a side-lacing ankle shoe and two types of closed ankle shoe. A piece broken from an upper with 'cut-out' decoration was also noted. Only shoe parts recovered during the Watching Brief were sufficiently well preserved for their styles to be recognisable and these may be dated to the early 15th century by comparison with the well dated material from the waterfront sites in the city of London (Grew and de Neergaard 1988).

The back part torn and cut from a side-lacing ankle shoe, SF23 (Fig 4.7, 18) was found along with an intersectional cutting piece, SF120, in dark silt [1328]. The calfskin ankle shoe, SF23, laced through a series of small, closely-spaced lace holes at the side of the foot; stitching present showed that these lace holes had been lined originally. The ankle shoe extended to lower calf height, a style that we would term an ankle boot today. Side-lace fastening shoes, Goubitz Type 50 variant I, were popular throughout the 13th, 14th and the first half of the 15th centuries (Goubitz *et al* 2001, 175); features such as the two quarters joining with a butted back seam on this example allow it to be dated to the 15th century (Grew and de Neergaard 1988:41-2) and this was by far the most common shoe style worn in capital city during the early 15th century (ibid, 43).

Parts from closed ankle shoes with two differing cutting patterns were found in dark silt (1434). A fragment torn from the left quarters of an ankle shoe with a curving front seam surviving to above ankle height, SF88.3, comes from an 'ankle boot' of a style also popular in the city of London in the early 15th century (Grew and de Neergaard 1988, 73, fig 107). The back part of a lower ankle shoe made with a one-piece upper of calfskin, SF129, came from the same deposit (1434) (Fig 4.7, 19). A slot for a narrow strap, no more than 8mm wide, suggests that the ankle shoe originally fastened with a strap and small metal buckle; another style popular at that time (ibid, 41) though it continued to be commonly worn through much of that century.

A small fragment torn from a shoe upper of calfskin, SF126, decorated with a series of punched circular holes, each 4mm in diameter, was amongst the shoe parts recovered from the dark silt (1434). This punched decoration, also known as openwork decoration, is occasionally found on shoes of various styles of both medieval and early post-medieval date. The circular motif found here is comparable with those on a vamp of a side-lacing shoe or low ankle shoe from the city of London, thought to date to the late 14th/early 15th centuries (Grew and de Neergaard 1988, 82, fig 116a). In this country such punched decoration is most often found on shoes of this date though an early example dates to the first half of the 13th century (ibid, 79). A wide range of punched motifs were used, see for example the variety decorating the medieval shoes from Dordrecht (Goubitz *et al* 2001, 47, fig 4).

Sixteenth-century footwear

Shoe leather of 16th-century date was recovered from four contexts (1186), (1187), (1323), (1333). Two fragments broken from large clump sole repairs, SF94, were found on a possible resurface of the Cathedral Square (1187). A midsole from a welted shoe with a broad, round toe, SF46, of adult male size and a second fragment broken from a welted shoe bottom component, SF51, were found in dark silt (1186) lying immediately above. These two deposits were dated to the 16th century and the leather present is contemporary. Welted shoe parts were recovered from two dark silts (1323), (1333) dating to the late 15th-16th centuries.

While many of the shoe parts were broken the group from (1333) included a complete welted sole of adult size, SF31, of broad, round-toed shape characteristic of 16th-century footwear and the right side of a vamp of cattle hide, SF30, with the side and throat cut away to salvage reusable leather. Also in (1333) with the leather were two lengths of copper alloy 'loop in loop' chain the individual links 6mm long and the wire less than 0.5mm thick. Two pieces of waste leather in the same deposit suggests the group to be cobbling waste.

Seventeenth-century footwear

Shoe leather of 17th-century date occurred in two silt deposits (806) and (1417). Components from bottom units of three welted shoes of adult size, SF20, 21, 22, and a fastening latchet, SF23, cut way from the quarters of a shoe upper of cattle hide were found in dark silt (806) dated to the late 16th-17th centuries. The oval-toed tread sole, SF22, made straight and gently moulded to extend for a small distance down a separate heel, and the wide, round-ended latchet, SF23, cut from a shoe that tied across the instep, are likely to come from shoes dating no earlier than the middle years of the 17th century. As two of the four pieces had secondary cutting the group appears to be cobbling waste.

The remains of three welted shoes were found in dark silt (1417) and dated to the 16th-17th centuries. The best preserved was part of a latchet tie-lace fastening welted shoe, SF38, of child size 7(24) with an upper of suede cattle hide (flesh side outward) that tied over a high tongue across the instep (Fig 4.7, 20). The vamp had been slit vertically down the centre presumably to improve the comfort for the wearer, perhaps when the shoe had been outgrown.

A second more fragmentary latchet tie-lace fastening shoe, SF122, of cattle hide was of slightly larger size, possibly for an adolescent being child size 11 (29), with a square-toed (chisel-pointed) insole. These two shoes had the impression of bracing thread present on their insoles and the larger, SF122, had pieces of rolled welt surviving indicating the type of common welted construction employed (Goubitz 1984, fig 5 no 8; Goubitz *et al* 2001, 285, fig 13b). A welted sole, SF121, came from a third shoe of similar size, child size *c*.11. All the shoes had been heavily worn and the two larger shoes, SF121 and SF122, had hobnailed soles and had been everyday working wear.

Bucket

A small piece of seam, SF124, broken from the base of a leather bucket was found in dark silt (1431) dating to the 16th century. Made of cattle hide, the moulded, closed seam had a double row of saddle stitching, stitch length 9mm, spaced 5mm apart. This small fragment of seam may be compared with those on the leather buckets on board the *Mary Rose* that sank in Portsmouth Harbour in 1545 (Mould and Cameron 2005).

Straps

The end of a strap with an angular iron buckle frame still attached, SF85 (Fig 4.6, 6) and a piece torn from a second length of strap, SF123, were found with shoes of 17th century date in dark silt (1417) dated to the 16th-17th centuries. The ends of the strap, SF85, 28mm (*c*.1 inch) wide, wrapped around the iron buckle and were held together by two lines of three iron rivets rather than the more usual saddle stitching, suggesting it had been used to take heavy strain. The second, narrower strap, SF123, varying from 22mm to 18mm wide, was stitched at the wider end and slit down the centre to take a buckle, with a series of six large buckle pin holes at the opposite end. The straps were made of cattle hide as is usually the case; the narrower, SF123, was notably robust being over 6mm thick.

Waste leather

Secondary waste produced when cutting out pattern pieces and trimming them to size during the manufacture and repair of leather goods were found in seven individual deposits. Three pieces of secondary waste trimmings of bovine leather including a paring cut from a skived (bevelled) edge were found along with medieval turnshoe parts in dark silt (05-15). A larger assemblage of waste leather was recovered coming from dark silt deposits dated to the 14th through to the 16th centuries.

The largest group, containing thirty pieces of secondary waste, SF127 and SF130.1-27, and two hide edges, SF130.28-9, known as primary waste, came from dark silt (1434) and were associated with turnshoes of earlier 15th-century date (see above). All were of bovine leathers; principally cattle hide with a small amount of calfskin also present. An intersectional cutting piece, SF83, produced when cutting out shoe soles, was found in (1328) with remains of a shoe of early 15th century date and another in (1333) with shoe parts of 16th century date, with a possible third example, SF64, from (1638) dated to the late 15th-16th centuries. One of trimmings of cattle hide, SF127.2, present in (1434) was also of distinctive shape having been cut away when trimming around the seat of a shoe sole. These pieces may provide a small amount of evidence that shoemaking as well as cobbling was being undertaken at this time, however, the refurbishing of old shoes including the adding of new soles to cut-down uppers was a feature of the cobbling trade, known as translation; and it may be more likely that this waste derives from that activity.

The leather from Cathedral Square in its local and regional context

Only a small amount of leather with a similar date range has been found in Peterborough previously. A very limited amount of shoe leather of early 15th, 16th and 17th century date was recognised during assessment of the material recovered from the excavations at 25/26 Long Causeway (Mould 1995) when an area of the town ditch was examined. Looking slightly further afield, a small number of shoes and other items of the same date were found during the excavations at the Grand Arcade, Cambridge in fills of the King's Ditch and pits located between 16/17 and 22 St Andrews Street (Mould 2009).

Late medieval leather is better represented with a group coming from Cumbergate located close to the Peterborough Cathedral Square. Shoes, straps and waste leather thought to be cobbling waste, was recovered from excavations at Queensgate on the site of medieval Cumbergate (Mould 2006, Fletcher and Mould 2010). These shoes were of styles current in the city of London during the late 14th and early 15th centuries. The majority of the leather was found in rubbish deposits securely dated to 1450-1500 and the suggestion was made that possibly the leather had been on a midden for some time before being deposited, presumably at the very beginning of that period. It is also possible that shoe styles continued to be worn in the provinces longer than they were in the capital or that the Queensgate group represents the clearance of belongings from a past generation. Only the recovery of footwear from other closely dated deposits outside the capital will help resolve this interesting conundrum.

The styles differ from those found at the Cathedral Square, and the Queensgate group appear to be slightly earlier in date. The Cathedral Square shoes can be dated by comparison with the well dated waterfront assemblages from the city of London to the first half of the 15th century (Grew and de Neergaard 1988) and, as such, would appear to be footwear belonging to the next generation of Peterborough folk.

Catalogue of illustrated leather

(Fig 4.7, 17-20)

17 Leather piece cut from a repaired turnshoe sole
    Sub-circular piece cut from the tread area of a turnshoe sole of adult size with two small areas of edge/flesh seam, stitch length 5mm, and heavily worn stitching to attach a repair clump present. Leather worn cattle hide 4.19mm thick. Length 76mm, width 75mm. SF128 (1434)

18 Leather side-lacing ankle shoe, right foot, adult size
    Left quarters with butted edge/flesh back seam, stitch length 3mm, whip stitched top edge and front opening with eleven small lace holes surviving, 2mm in diameter and 10mm apart. Whip stitching from a lapped seam mark the former position of a lace hole lining and a heel stiffener. Fragment of matching right quarters with cut and torn edges, the top of a heel stiffener and four small upper fragments (not illustrated). Quarters *c.*156mm high at centre back, 60mm wide, leather worn bovine probably calfskin 2.58mm; heel stiffener bovine 1.96mm thick. SF23 (1328) conduit trench

19 Leather part of a one-piece ankle shoe, left foot, adult size
    Back part of ankle shoe with a one-piece upper, the lasting margin worn away at centre back. Plain cut top edge with the vertical edge/flesh butted side seam 88mm high, stitch length 3.5mm, survives on the left side, other edges torn away. A double slit for a narrow fastening strap and whip stitching from a lapped seam present at the top of the side seam marking the former position of a tongue and a fastening strap. A heel stiffener, *c.*70mm high, placed at centre back, grain side outward to the foot. Upper estimated *c.*105mm high at centre back, leather calfskin 1.82mm thick; heel stiffener possibly pigskin 2.37mm thick. SF129 (1434)

20 Leather welted latchet-tying shoe, straight, child size
    Insole with blunt, oval toe, medium tread, waist and seat with edge/flesh seam, stitch length 7mm. The impression of bracing thread is visible on the flesh side (underside). The vamp (still attached to the insole) is worn away at the toe and covered with a straight toe cap, and heavily worn down the left side. It has sloping butted edge/grain side seams, stitch length 3mm, 40mm high, and a high, slightly flaring, straight-ended tongue with a pair of fastening holes. A secondary slit runs vertically between the fastening holes down to the toe. Leather vamp cattle hide flesh outward 2.39mm thick; toe cap worn bovine 1.45mm thick. Insole length 158mm, width tread 52mm waist 36mm, seat 42mm. Child size 7(24). SF38 (1417)

Ceramic building material
by Pat Chapman

Brick

There are 220 bricks, comprising nine complete examples and 211 fragments of varying sizes.

Many of the bricks are handmade examples, often pale red to mauve, cindery from being slightly over fired, or with yellow streaks, while orange, orange-brown and red-brown bricks are also quite common, with a few dark purple examples. These bricks would have been produced locally. A few yellow bricks, including a perforated example, which began to be used from the late 18th century onwards either as Dutch imports or made in areas with Gault clay. There are more modern complete bricks, one stamped with STAR in one frog, probably either manufactured by the Dogsthorpe Star Brick Co or the Star Pressed Brick Co, local companies of the late 19th and early 20th centuries.

There are also two white glazed bricks from the toilet block in the 1893 extension of the Corn Exchange building. They come from Halifax, one stamped with HALIFAX, and the other stamped HALIFAX on one side and the other side with OATES & GREEN LTD, a company specialising in urinals and the construction of toilet blocks (Fig 4.8).

The dimensions of the complete bricks are given in Table 4.4. Earlier brick fragments are typically 54-60mm thick and up to 120mm, both thinner and wider than the more modern varieties.

Most of the bricks retain either lime mortar adhering to one or more surfaces, or Portland cement dating from the mid-19th century.

This assemblage indicates the great variety in the colour of bricks that were used in the more vernacular buildings from at least the 16th century until the early 20th century.

Ceramic roof tile

There are 218 ceramic roof tile sherds. These are virtually all flat tiles, plain or glazed green or yellow. Four tiles have round pegholes, another four have nibs. There are also eleven examples of green glazed and plain

The History and Archaeology of Cathedral Square Peterborough

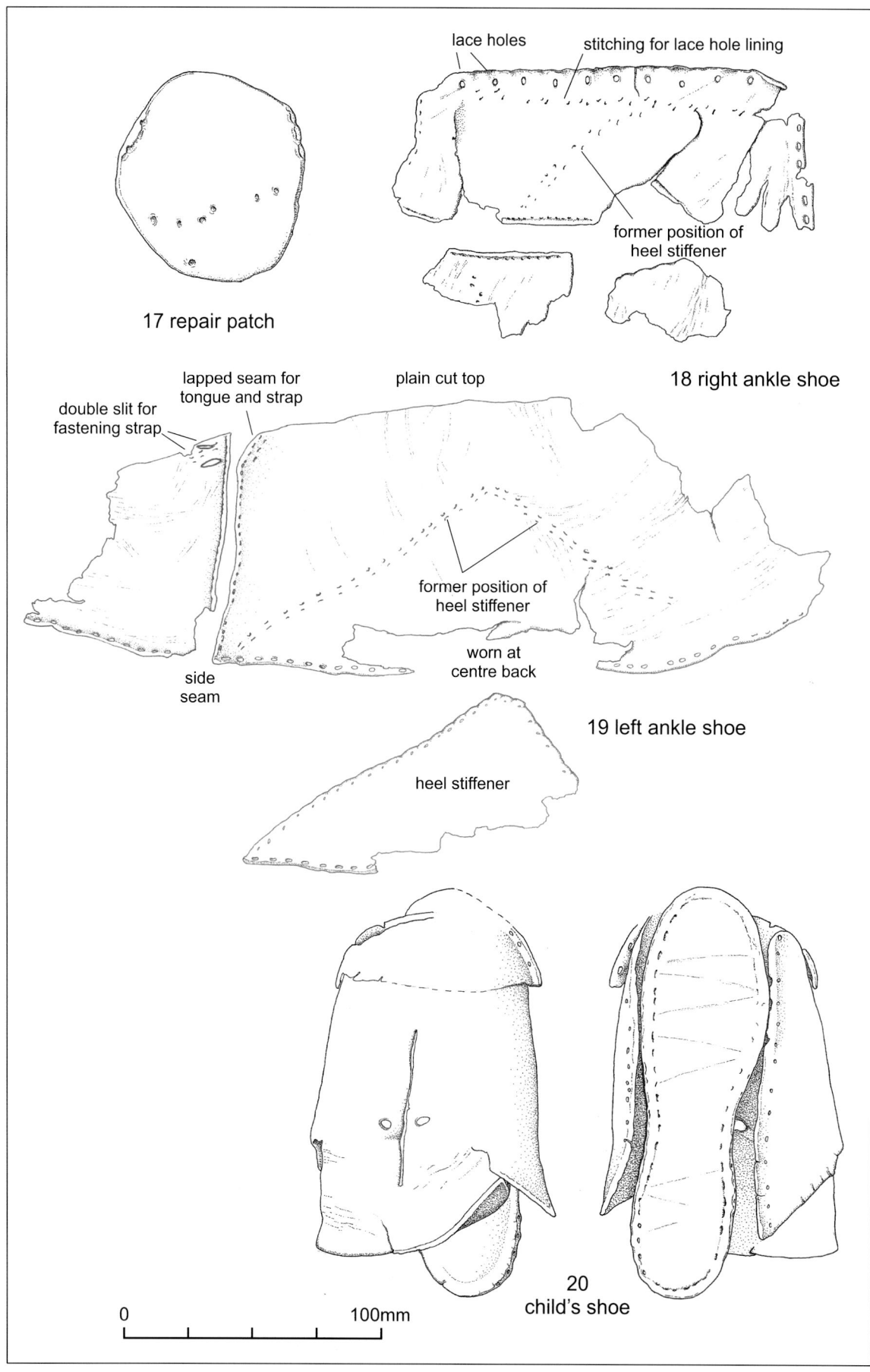

Fig 4.7: Leather shoes (17-20)

3. The Archaeology of Cathedral Square

Fig 4.8: Oates and Green brick (left), Halifax (right) and local Star brick (below)

Context/type	Size (mm)	Description
1501 cellar/toilet wall, Corn Exchange extension	225 x 110 x 72 225 x 110 x 72	White, white glazed stretcher HALIFAX White, white glazed header, OATES & GREEN LTD HALIFAX on reverse
1505 demolition from Corn Exchange	223 x 105 x 65 215 x 105 x 50 220 x 100 x 55 220 x 105 x 70	STAR
1514, Corn Exchange cellar	220 x 105 x 55 220 x 105 x 55	Yellow, horizontal skintling Pinkish, rough,
1525, wall	220 x 112 x 65	Yellow

Table 4.4: Dimensions of complete bricks

roof ridge tiles and four remnant crests. One tile has the ubiquitous dog paw print.

The tiles are typically 11-15mm thick. One flat tile sherd is 165mm wide or 6½ inches, which was the standard width demanded by Act of Parliament in 1477. Three sherds are 180-183mm wide (7¼ inches) and one is 200mm wide (8 inches). The only measurable length is in excess of 285mm (11¼ inches), longer than the standard 10½ inches (265mm).

The fabric for most of the tiles is coarse to fine orange-brown to red-brown clay, often with a grey core. This is typical of the Lyveden-Stanion ware, both villages produced roof tiles as well as pottery, and the tiles would be predominantly dated from the 14th century to the early 16th century. Two of the ridge tile crests, a small pyramid and part of an anvil shape were found in Stanion (Chapman 2008). A few tiles are well made and could either be later in date or from a different source.

There are no pantiles, which date from the late 17th century onwards, or more modern machine-made tiles. This lack suggests that the roof tile assemblage is medieval to early post-medieval in date, coming from buildings of similar date. If there had been more modern tiles they had been saved for reuse or they were not collected.

Ceramic floor tile

There are 16 sherds of floor tile, from medieval to modern in date. Twelve tiles are medieval to early post-medieval in date. These are typically in a coarse orange fabric with a grey core, with one made in a fine pink fabric, one red-brown and two that have been cut to triangles were fired to black. Four of the tiles are green glazed. The only medieval tile from the churchyard area had white slip under the glaze, there is a remnant design, but it is too badly worn to determine the pattern.

The remaining four tiles are late 19th century to modern in date. Two of these are brick-like paviers worn smooth. The other two tiles could have been used as wall tiles; one is plain with a stamped grid on the back for adhering to mortar or cement and the other tile, is a complete 6 inches square (150mm) with the name EXCELSIOR stamped within a circle, possibly from W & P Jones, Jackfield in Shropshire.

These few tiles are just the remnants left that indicate that plain and glazed floor tiles were used during the medieval period, with a change to brick-like paviers at a later date.

Mortar and plaster

There are 878 fragments of varying sizes of mortar and plaster, weighing 3.64kg. While some of these fragments are plaster and some mortar, there are also some that are not readily definable. Most of these fragments are of white lime, while a few are grey Portland cement.

Of the obvious plaster remains, 91 fragments weighing 2.24kg, some have wattle or combing impressions, indicating their structural use.

The remaining 787 fragments, weighing 1.40kg, have been categorised as mortar. This includes those from (1756-1759), labelled as mortar floor.

The plaster remains indicate that some of the buildings at least were wattle or lath and plaster, and some of the plaster may have been decorated. The fragments of grey Portland cement would date from the mid-19th century onwards and could have been used in repairs to older houses or for new buildings.

Clay tobacco-pipes
by Tora Hylton

A group of 144 clay tobacco-pipe fragments were recovered during the excavations. The assemblage comprises 21 complete or fragmented pipe-bowls and 123 stem fragments. Many of the pipe fragments display signs of abrasion and a small number of bowls appear to be partially blackened on their internal surfaces, suggesting that they had been used.

Fourteen bowls are sufficiently complete to enable dating, following Oswald's simplified typology using bowl and foot/spur forms (1975, 37-41). The earliest bowl form represented is Oswald's Type G5, which dates to c.1640-60. Just one example was recovered, from the dark silt deposits underlying the Corn Exchange, together with four other examples representing Oswald's type G6, G17 and G18. The majority of datable bowls provide a closely dated range of c.1660-1680 and most of these were recovered from deposits dated by the pottery to the 18th century, suggesting that these deposits also incorporated material of 17th century date.

The assemblage is dominated by five examples of Oswald's Type G17 and six examples of Type G18. All the bowls are unmarked, therefore cannot be attributed to an individual maker. The majority of bowls and stems are burnished and all the bowls are ornamented with a partial or complete milled band/groove set just below the lip of the bowl, a common motif until c.1710 (Moore 1980, 6); There is one 18th-century pipe bowl, Oswald's Type G10, which were recovered from 18th-century makeup deposits (1715) and dates to 1700-40. Finally one bowl fragment is decorated with vertical striations and relief moulded leaves along the front seam of the bowl, stylistically it dates to the 19th century.

There are 123 stem fragments which measure up to 100mm in length. One fragment retains a flat ended mouthpiece and signs of wear are vaguely evident at the terminal.

The animal bone
by Karen Deighton

A total of 27.25kg of animal bone was collected by hand from a range of contexts during the course of excavation. This material was analysed to determine the level of preservation and the taxa present. The contribution to the understanding of the economy, status and function of the site was also considered.

The material was sorted into recordable and non-recordable fragments. Quantification followed Halstead after Watson (1979) and used minimum anatomical element (Min. A.U). The following were recorded for each element: context, anatomical element, taxa, proximal fusion and distal fusion, side, preservation, fragmentation, modification, butchery evidence and sex (where appropriate). Vertebra and ribs (with articulating ends) were counted and noted as small or large ungulate but not included in quantification. Epiphyseal fusion follows Silver (1969). Ovicaprid teeth were aged after Payne (1973), cattle after Halstead (1985) and pigs after Bull and Payne (1982). Recognition of butchery is after Binford (1981). Material from sieved samples was also included, mesh sizes were 3.4mm, 1mm and 500microns.

The animal bone assemblage

Fragmentation was heavy with only 16.7% of bone being whole; this was largely the result of old breaks (Table 4.5). Fragmentation was possibly the result of heavy-handed butchery techniques as suggested by the frequency of evidence for chopping (see below). However, trampling should not be ruled out as a cause of heavy fragmentation as most bone is from the dark silt layer which covers the site. Bone surface abrasion was average, although some flaking was observed. Black-brown staining consistent with waterlogging was noted on material from dark silts (1333), (1366), (1477) and (1733). Canid gnawing was noted on 80 bones, 25.8%, and further attests to the presence of dogs and could suggest bone lay exposed after disposal, further evidence to support to support trampling as the reason for the high level of fragmentation. Furthermore, a high frequency of canid gnawing could also result in preservation bias against smaller bones and smaller taxa.

3. The Archaeology of Cathedral Square

Fragment type	Number	Percentage
Whole	42	16.7%
End+shaft	46	18.3%
Cylinder	38	15.1%
Splinter	22	8.7%
Some shaft missing	87	34.6%
End	8	3.1%
End+shaft	6	2.3%
Fresh break	2	0.7%
Total	251	100

TABLE 4.5: ANIMAL BONE FRAGMENTATION

A total of 78 butchery marks were noted, 72 were the result of chopping and evidence for skinning, sawing, dismembering and filleting was also noted. One cattle humerus was split longitudinally. No evidence of burning was noted, suggesting that this was not a preferred method of disposal. A metal fragment embedded in the proximal articulation of a cattle radius was noted from context (1434). One antler showed the removal of tines from the branch and the burr had apparently been roughly chopped to remove it from the skull.

Species present

Tables 4.6-4.8 summarise the animal species present.

Cattle were the dominant taxa. These were utilised for meat, milk, traction and hides. Sheep/goat were utilised for meat, milk and wool. Pigs were utilised for meat but could be kept in an urban setting and fed on household waste, this scenario could be tentatively suggested for the current site by the presence of piglet remains in context (1434). Horses were mostly used for traction and transport, the consumption of horse flesh had been outlawed by papal bull, however, knackering for hides, bones (for glue) and food for hounds was still practiced. Although dogs filled many roles such as guarding, hunting, companion animal and herding, their presence here is just as likely to be as stray animals. Dog fur was also utilised. The presence of deer bone as well as antler could suggest high status as hunting deer was the preserve of the nobility. However, poaching was not unknown. Cats were often feral but played a role in pest control as well as being used for fur. Domestic fowl was utilised for feathers, meat and eggs and often kept in an urban environment. Goose was mostly used for meat and feathers.

Ageing and sexing

Both toothwear and epiphyseal fusion data were available for ageing, but there is no sexing data.

Toothwear data is more reliable for ageing, but not enough was available to analyse any kill-off patterns. However, it can be tentatively suggested that cattle were killed at an optimum age for beef production (see below), which might be the expected result from a market place containing Butchers Row, but little more can be said of animal husbandry (Table 4.9).

Pathologies

A cattle phalange 3 from (1417) had exotosis (excess bone growth) covering the entire proximal articulation and a third of the front and sides. Exotosis and roughening were noted around a cattle acetabulum from the same context. Exotosis is often a symptom of arthritic conditions and can suggest old age or use of the animal for traction. Finally, from (1417) a sheep mandible with uneven wear on the fourth permanent premolar and interdental attrition was observed.

Taxon	cattle	sheep/goat	pig	horse	deer	dog	cat	Small ungulate	Large ungulate
Total	235	203	29	14	5	6	2	8	32
Percentage	47.8%	39.3%	6.1%	2.1%	1.3%	1.1%	0.5%	N/A	N/A

TABLE 4.6: MAMMALS PRESENT

Element	domestic fowl	goose	bird
Total	4	8	4
Percentage	0.5%	0.5%	0.5%

TABLE 4.7: BIRDS PRESENT

Taxon	Cattle	Sheep/goat	Pig	Horse	Rabbit	Large ungulate	Small ungulate	Domestic fowl	Bird indet.	amphibian	Fish indet
Total	7	11	3	1	3	2	2	1	8	1	4

TABLE 4.8: ANIMAL BONE FROM DARK SILT SIEVED SAMPLES

Context	Taxa	Element	Side	TWS	Approximate age
1333	cattle	mandible	R	D	18-30 months
1343	cattle	mandible	L	D+	18-30 months+
1417	cattle	mandible	L	C+	8-18 months+
1417	cattle	mandible	R	C+	8-18 months+
1434	cattle	M3	L	E	30-36 months
1333	S/G	mandible	R	F	3-4 years
1417	S/G	mandible	R	C	6-12 months
1417	S/G	mandible	L	I	8-10 years
1417	S/G	mandible	R	I	8-10 years
1417	S/G	mandible	R	I	8-10 years
1434	S/G	mandible	R	D+	1-2 years+
1434	S/G	mandible	R	E	2-3 years
1414	pig	mandible	R	C	6-13 months
1434	pig	mandible	L	A	0-7 weeks

TABLE 4.9: TOOTH ERUPTION AND WEAR OF MAIN DOMESTICATES

Discussion

Body part analysis was only possible for cattle and sheep/goat. A similar pattern is seen for both taxa. The low frequency of the by-products of primary butchery (ie axis, atlas, mandibles and phalanges) suggests that meat arrived at the site as dressed carcasses or joints, therefore indicating the genesis of the assemblage to be kitchen waste. Closer scrutiny reveals that bone frequencies follow the general pattern for frequency of bone elements, increasing with increasing utility up to and including proximal humeri; beyond this point frequency drops sharply which suggests a preference for cuts of meat from the forelimbs. The pattern cannot be attributed to preservation bias as elements such as proximal and distal humerus which are well represented at the site are not usually well preserved.

Comparisons with other medieval and post-medieval urban sites in the city and regionally is limited by the relatively small size of the assemblage. The averaging effect of the broad time period to which the assemblage relates is also problematic for intersite comparisons.

Plant macrofossils
by Karen Deighton

The material was analysed to determine the level of preservation, the taxa present and the contribution to the understanding of the economy and function of the site. Phasing follows Steve Morris (pers comm) and suggests a single broad phase covering the 12th to late 17th centuries.

The samples were processed using a modified siraf tank fitted with a 250micron mesh and flot sieve. The resulting flots and residues were dried. The flots were then sorted with the aid of a stereoscopic microscope (10x magnification) and residues were scanned. Any charred plant remains were identified with the aid of the author's reference collection (Cappers et al 2006, Jacomet 1996, Schoch et al 1988 and the SCRI website).

Preservation by both charring and waterlogging was seen. Seeds and grains exhibited a low level of fragmentation and surface abrasion. Most specimens could be identified to taxa (Table 4.10).

All samples were dominated by waterlogged wood and/or charcoal fragments which is probably cumulative detritus. The presence of any seeds or grains seems to be the result of casual disposal. The occurrence of charred cereal grains is possibly due to accidental burning during final preparation for use or storage. The presence of various fruit seeds provides some evidence of dietary preference. The incidence of grape pips could indicate foreign trade and the consumption of luxury goods. Seeds of the wild/weed taxa (eg buttercup, fat hen) are all waterlogged which suggests these taxa grew on local waste ground. Due to the paucity of data and the broad phasing intersite comparisons were not feasible. Analysis has provided some evidence of dietary preference and the local environment during the medieval and post-medieval period.

A large proportion of the silt layer was certainly organic and highly pungent, probably derived from animal excrement and the blood and waste from the butchery of the animals themselves. No doubt a proportion of household and human waste also ended up on the square and streets as well, adding to the already unsanitary conditions. The surface although solid in dry conditions must have been intolerable in wet winter conditions, which reflects on the governing authority's inability or negligence to improve the situation.

The building in the south-east corner of the square, may have been used as a public building and may have had a series of garden or yard surfaces, from which the evidence may also resolve the function of the structures.

Marine shells
by Karen Deighton

A total of 1.1kg of marine shells was recovered from a range of contexts. This material was analysed to provide information on preservation and taxa present.

The assemblage comprised 82 oyster shell fragments (52 upper and 30 lower), 19 cockles and 32 mussels. Fragmentation and abrasion were moderate. Two possible instances of butchery were noted, an upper oyster valve and a cockle shell had holes through them. Some evidence of ornamentation was observed on the oyster shells in the form of slight ribbing.

The presence of marine species indicates trade with the coast. The small size of the oysters and the presence of shell attachments suggest the oysters were wild gathered as opposed to farmed. The presence of some ornamentation could indicate that the oysters grew in shallow water as ornamentation usually occurs in the presence of sunlight.

Context: dark silts		613	1016	1186	1186	1214	1222	1186	1454
Sample		1	1	5	6	8	9	10	15
Volume	Totals	40	40	40	40	40	40	40	40
Hulled Barley, Hordeum vulgare	10	-	4	2	-	1	3	-	-
Naked Barley, Hodeum vulgare var nudum	17	-	8	3	-	-	6	-	-
Rye Secale cereale	1	1	-	-	-	-	-	-	-
Cereal indet	8	1	6	-	-	-	1	-	-
Grape, Vitis vinifera	3	-	-	1	-	2	-	-	-
Raspberry, Rubus idaeus	1	-	1	-	-	-	-	-	-
Blackberry, Rubus fruticosus	1	-	-	-	-	1	-	-	-
Pos pear, (Pyrus sp)	1	-	-	-	-	1	-	-	-
Plum, Pruncus domestica	2	-	-	-	2	-	-	-	-
Elder, Sambucus sp	4	-	1	-	1	-	1	1	-
Buttercup, Rununculus sp	21	-	3	4	1	5	-	1	7
Fat hen, Chenopodium album	6	-	-	4	-	-	1	-	1
Sheep sorrel, Rumex acetosella	1	-	-	1	-	-	-	-	-
Dock type, Rumex sp	1	-	1	-	-	-	-	-	-
Bistort, Persicaria sp	1	-	-	-	-	1	-	-	-
Small pulse, Brassica sp	2	-	1	1	-	-	-	-	-
Indet	2	-	1	1	-	-	-	-	-
Hazelnut, Corylus sp	1	-	-	-	-	1	-	-	-
Total		2	26	17	4	12	12	2	8

TABLE 4.10: PLANT MACROFOSSILS, TAXA PRESENT

5. Discussion

Here is a plentiful market on Saturday, which is well stored with the best of meat, fish, and fowl, wild and tame, and at more reasonable prices than at many neighbouring markets. Fruit is, in general, plentiful and cheap.

There are two chartered fairs; the first by King Richard, upon the feast of St. Peter, for eight days, but now contracted to two, on the 10th and 11th of July, which is most noted for home-spun cloth, beasts, horses, wood, haberdashery, and toys: the second fair, chartered by King Henry the Sixth, is called Brigg Fair, holden on the 2nd and 3rd of October.

The manufactures here consist of all kinds of hosiery; but its export trade has arisen from large quantities of malt and corn sent down the river. Its imports are mostly coals, and groceries for the consumption of the inland country.

Topography of Great Britain, 1802-29, George Alexander Cooke

Introduction

The excavations in Cathedral Square represent perhaps the most extensive archaeological investigation undertaken to date within the medieval core of Peterborough. However, the nature of the investigations, primarily as a long-term watching brief, have somewhat limited detailed analysis of the origins of the market place and its subsequent evolution. Many of the individual interventions did not penetrate significantly into the underlying archaeological horizons and when this did occur, the area was small and access was often restricted. In all there were over 130 separate interventions that were archaeologically recorded. The almost continuous presence of a single person, Stephen Morris, throughout the entire development, and his fundamental understanding of the overall stratigraphy of the area, has enabled these disparate interventions to be correlated to provide the narrative presented in Chapter 3.

Despite the somewhat limited nature of the material evidence, large-scale excavations of market places within the country have been comparatively rare. Of the excavations that have taken place, the evidence is often poor, with earlier surfaces truncated or removed entirely by later modernisation. Excavations at the market place in Norwich, Norfolk for instance, showed that it had been significantly remodelled in around 1500 and no archaeological remains earlier than the late 15th century survived (Norfolk HER no 40773; heritage.norfolk.gov.uk/).

Similarly, post-medieval remodelling of the market place at Darlington, County Durham had truncated any earlier deposits (Archaeological Services 2008). However, excavations undertaken at Ripon, North Yorkshire in 2001 found evidence for market place features dating from the 13th century, revealing similar sequences of deposition as at Peterborough (Archaeological Services 2011). The excavations at Peterborough have therefore provided significant information regarding the development and evolution of a provincial market.

Origins and development

Surviving evidence in the area of the market place prior to the Saxo-Norman period was limited to a large pit and a posthole, neither of which are dated, but which were sealed beneath the earliest market place surface and are therefore likely to pre-date its creation, which is thought to have occurred in the mid-12th century (Mackreth 1994). The absence of buried soils suggests that there was widespread levelling and soil stripping prior to the laying of the early market place; this is likely to have destroyed more ephemeral evidence and it is unlikely that any pre-market place features would have penetrated significantly beneath the uppermost ground levels.

There was no evidence for any quarry pits dating to the Saxon to Saxo-Norman period, as observed during excavations at The Still to the north (Spoerry and Hinman 1998). While this apparent lack of pre-market place activity may in part be a result of the few deeper interventions, there was little pottery dating to the period pre-1150 found residually in later features, while excavations at The Still found significant quantities. This may suggest that the area later taken in by the market place was marginal to any settlement or other activity prior to its creation.

The origin of settlement to the west of the monastery has been the subject of some debate. While it is generally agreed that there was an early market-place located to the north-east of the *burh* at Bondgate/Boongate, Professor King suggested that there was another area of settlement to the west of the monastery prior to the founding of the 'new town' and that this was likely to have dated from 1070 at the latest, when sixty knights were imposed on the monastery by King William, following the Hereward uprising (King 1981). However, Mackreth has argued that settlement on the western side of the monastery was created as part of the 'new town' in the mid-12th century, and as such was planned expansion of the existing settlement (Mackreth 1994). The medieval street plan, with its generally sub-rectangular morphology, is suggestive of such a planned expansion.

While the investigations at Cathedral Square provided little opportunity to observe pre-market place activity, the comparative absence of late Saxon and Saxo-Norman artefacts, even as residual material, tends to suggest that this area was likely to have been marginal land until the mid-12th century, giving more credence to Mackreth's theory of development.

The market place

The Abbot of the monastery at Peterborough held the right to hold a Saturday market under a charter of Edgar, founder of the second monastery in the 10th century. This may have originally been the market at Boongate to the north-east of the monastery, subsequently moving to its current location in the 12th century. The Abbot and Convent controlled the market during the medieval period and from 1315 was additionally granted the right to levy a pavage on all goods brought for sale within the *vill* (Mellows 1939). There were no trade or craft guilds in the town, rather trade was regulated by the Abbot's bailiff, who ran the Court of Pie Powder, which oversaw the market and its traders, hence only religious guilds were present.

After Dissolution, the Dean and Chapter were confirmed in the City of Peterborough and in their other estates all the powers formerly exercised by the Abbot. This included the right to hold the markets and two fairs, of which one, known as St Peter's or the Cherry Fair, was held in the market place. While the Dean and Chapter still owned the market, it along with many other elements of the estate, were leased out. Edgar's charter, confirmed by Elizabeth, decreed that *there be a market in Peterborough, and that there be none other betwixt Stamford and Huntingdon*. Peterborough was, therefore, the dominant market town within a radius of some 10-15 miles during the medieval period. Traders coming into the market in the 16th century are recorded from various settlements including Whittlesey, Market Deeping, Castor and even as far as Cowbit and Spalding, 16 miles to the north. In 1562, the Dean and Chapter, citing the terms of the charter, tried to suppress a market at Yaxley, just over four miles to the south, but it was decided that the inhabitants could keep a market on Thursday between the feast of Purification and Pentecost. However, a hundred years later it had been entirely suppressed (VCH 1936).

The Peterborough Feoffees were established in 1572 with the task of overseeing the lands formerly belonging to the guilds and parish of St John the Baptist. The tasks of the new body were, in general, of a charitable nature, but also included the repair of the church, certain buildings and highways north of the river. Over the decades their sphere of influence appears to have broadened, but with simultaneous neglect, with the result that a commission was appointed to inquire into their conduct in the early 17th century.

The investigations were dominated by the sequence of market place surfaces, the earliest of which is thought to date to the mid-12th century, although there were few artefacts predating the 14th-15th centuries. The surfaces were successively subsumed by layers of organic black silts, deriving from the disposal of refuse by the people using and living by the market. Much of this refuse appears to have originated from rather malodorous processes; one of the worst offenders, mentioned time and again over the centuries, appears to have been the butchery trade.

The early management of the market place was undertaken by the monastery and there is little evidence, either historically or archaeologically, for this earlier period. The accumulation of refuse seems to have reached its peak in the 16th century following Dissolution and there are repeated instances of people being fined for various offences. In 1575 Michael Edmundes had left a dead dog in the market place for a week, while Thomas Surflet had at least twice allowed a *heape of earth and myre* to encroach onto the marketstead, other, lesser offences, included the emptying of chamber pots into the street (Mellows and Gifford 1956).

Records pertaining to the improvement and maintenance of the roads and pavements are numerous from the 16th century or so, but suggest that it was generally undertaken as a piecemeal operation until the late 18th century. Subsequent to the Dissolution, the Dean and Chapter were responsible for their upkeep, although after to 1548, there is no mention of road improvement in the accounts. The maintenance and upkeep was later a responsibility of the Feoffees. Documents relating to the repair of the market place in 1623-6, record payments for loads of 'pibble' brought into the city via the Gunworth (ie Milton) Ferry, as well as loads of cobble and gravel. The location of the pits used to gather these materials is not known, but are likely to have been located at Fletton and on the Common (Mellows 1937). Further 'paving of the Market Hill' was undertaken in 1628 following a gift of £5 from the newly elected MP for the city. These successive repairs probably account for the significant make-up layers observed during the excavation across the market place.

While late 17th-century resurfacing of the market place appears to have halted much of the encroachment of the black silts, the market square only seems to have become an area free of filth in the late 18th century with the formation of the Peterborough Pavement and Improvement Commission in 1790.

The encroachment of filth does not appear to have been confined to Peterborough by any means. While there have been relatively few excavations within market places; the build-up of this type of deposit has been noted elsewhere. Excavations at Ripon Market Place revealed a similar sequence of deposits; the first formal market place surface there was dated to around the 14th to 15th centuries and comprised a bedding layer of sand, over which a rather undulating layer of cobbles was laid. Almost as soon as this surface was laid down a layer of organic black silt appears to have started to accumulate. Within the layer were large amounts of pottery, bone, wood and leather. Test pits dug within Boston market place found black organic silts containing medieval and post-medieval finds (Cope-Faulkner 2010).

Artefacts and trade

The majority of the artefacts, including the pottery, date from the 15th-16th centuries onwards and were largely found incorporated into the dark silts overlying the market square surfaces. The lack of earlier material probably reflects the continuous process of deposition and trampling, with perhaps intermittent episodes of at least partial clearance of the market place surface during the period following its creation in the 12th century and later burial by subsequent surfaces from the 16th century onwards. Artefacts recovered from stratified contexts were rare and prevented detailed dating and analysis of features. However, some assemblages were significant in their own right despite the lack of context.

The artefact assemblage provided little evidence for zoning, that is, the specific areas within the market place allocated for each trade; it is likely that the churning of the dark silt deposits gradually spread the rubbish discarded by traders over a wide area.

Butchers Row, which survived until the mid-19th century, was latterly located to the west of the Church of St John the Baptist, but the butchers' shambles had existed in this area prior to the construction of the church in the early 1400s. Butter, eggs and milk were traditionally sold under the Butter Cross in the centre of the market and the fish market appears to have been located in the south-eastern corner of the market place. Peterborough market appears to have attracted its fair share of poor traders and a wealth of documentation details their transgressions, particularly the fish and meat traders from outside the town.

In 1575, the Nokes of Ramsey were fined for selling *naughtyefische* and at various times butchers were presented at court for selling *naughty beefe* and *messeld pork* (Mellows and Gifford 1956). Butchers were only allowed to sell meat in Butchers Row and, again, it was butchers from outside the town who attempted bypass this by hawking meat in the streets. At the Easter court of 1582, no fewer than three butchers were presented for this.

The dominance of locally-produced wares used and sold within the market is illustrated by the large quantity of Bourne D Ware found across the excavation, which contributed more than half of the entire assemblage by weight. Clearly, the industry at Bourne had created a virtual monopoly within the town for workaday vessels until its collapse in 1637 after a catastrophic fire at the kilns. Other local industries were also represented, particularly from Glapthorn to the west, but with little material originating from production centres to the east and south-east of the town, a trend noted previously (Spoerry and Hinman 1998). Specialist vessels included a possible cucurbit, a type of bowl used for collecting residues or salts and undecorated Tin Glazed Earthenware, which together may suggest the presence of a druggist or apothecary nearby during the 17th or 18th century. There were relatively few imported vessels, but notable amongst the examples are two Westerwald-types, the production of which commenced in 1665.

The assemblage of shoe leather dated from the early 15th century through to the 17th century and was from the dark silts. The late medieval assemblage was concentrated in the north-eastern part of the market square, with the largest single group from the junction with Long Causeway. Shoe leather has previously been found in small amounts during an investigation at 25/26 Long Causeway and in larger quantities on Cumbergate (Casa-Hatton *et al* 2007). The Cumbergate assemblage, though earlier than the current assemblage, also appeared to be the product of the cobbling trade. Adjacent excavation at The Still found no leather.

The shoe leather appears in the main to be waste from the cobbling trade rather than the shoe-making trade and the distribution suggests that cobblers were likely to be situated in the north-eastern part of the square, into Long Causeway and Cumbergate. Later, in the 16th century, pieces were again found in the eastern part of the square, but the only 17th-century fragments were found in two contexts in Queen Street to the west, perhaps suggesting that the focus of cobbling in the late medieval period had moved by the 17th century.

The bone and plant macrofossil assemblages were surprisingly poor, given the likely origin of much of the dark silt deposits. The bone assemblage does not appear to have been derived from primary butchery of animal carcasses given the absence of key skeletal elements, suggesting that it was derived largely from a domestic, rather than trade, source. Given the make-up of the assemblage, bone waste from Butchers Row, on the western side of the market place, appears to have been disposed of elsewhere. Certainly no significant dumps of bone were identified. The assemblage is typically dominated by cattle and sheep/goat and tooth wear analysis suggests that the cattle were being slaughtered at prime ages for beef production. Other bones indicated wealthier eating habits, including those of goose and deer. There were also a number of fish bones, as well as oyster, mussel and cockle shells; the fish market was apparently located at the south-eastern corner of the market and probably sold a variety of fresh and either salted or dried fish, sold as 'stockfish', both from saltwater and freshwater sources. Dried and salt fish was distributed from Boston and Lynn markets throughout the Midlands by both cart and boat; it is likely that that being sold at Peterborough came via the Nene.

There were a number of commonly available fruit within the plant macrofossil assemblage, including plum, pear, raspberry, blackberry and elder. While some of these fruits may have been grown in orchards, such as the pear, others, in particular the blackberry and elder, were likely to have been collected from hedgerows or local areas of scrubland. The hazelnut may have been similarly collected. Grapes on the other hand are likely to have been imported as raisins or currants from Spain or Portugal. While there is evidence of viticulture in the country, this seems to have declined in the 14th and 15th centuries, with little evidence after this period (Grieg 1996).

There were relatively few items that could be directly associated with specific trades within the market place. A small number of trade tokens and jettons were found; both essential elements of the market economy.

A cloth seal, probably from a clothier or weaver, was found on a floor surface in Building 3 along with a pair of shears and may provide some indication of the type of trade that was being undertaken in that space.

The finds evidence, though dominated by artefacts from the 16th to 17th centuries when the general upkeep of the market place appears to have been at its worst, appears to point to an economy primarily based around locally produced foodstuffs and general goods, with few more luxurious or imported items. Peterborough market, during both the medieval and post-medieval periods, seems to have been dominated by a typically provincial economy. Traders recorded coming into town during the post-medieval period seem to have been primarily from the surrounding villages and towns. The town was located to the east of the main north-south roads, which crossed the Nene at Castor, and, later, at Wansford, so was located some distance from passing trade over land. However, William Morton, who was the almoner of Peterborough Abbey in the late 15th century, records a great range of goods coming to the monastery via the river, including thatch, bricks and hay (King 1981).

In the medieval period in particular the town was likely eclipsed by the important markets located on the Wash to the east, notably Boston and (Kings) Lynn, as well as Stamford to the west, which was noted for its cloth manufacture and St Ives to the south, also noted for cloth (Carus-Wilson 1962). Though the ports of Boston and Lynn declined dramatically in importance during the later Middle Ages and beyond, they continued to import a wide range of consumer goods, likely destined for the wider hinterland. However, the artefact assemblage recovered at Peterborough does not appear to reflect a ready supply of foreign imported goods.

Structures on the market place

The remains of a range of different structures were identified during the project. Two walls of a building on the eastern side of the market place may relate to the Chapel of St Thomas, which was demolished in the early 15th century. Fragmentary remains of a building in the location of the former Sexton's House included three of four floor layers of clay and mortar, as well as the remains of a medieval mortar which was set into the base of the earliest floor and possibly used as a urinal. The remainder of the building was truncated. Furthermore, there were no associated finds apart from the mortar which was 13th or 14th century in origin. Although a re-used piece, it is tempting to suggest that the floors relate to a building that pre-dated the construction of Church of St John the Baptist in the early 15th century, demolished as part of that development, or one built at around the same period. It is likely that the building was associated with the butchers' trade as this was the traditional location of the shambles, even prior to the construction of the church. The construction of the church was a significant loss of area within the market and must have necessitated major re-organisation of trader's stalls and shops.

The most substantial remains were those of Building 3, occupying the eastern part of the market place during the 16th and 17th centuries; further remains in the same area included those of a possible market cross. Immediately south of the cathedral gateway, were remains of buildings demolished when Bridge Street was widened in the first half of the 20th century. A series of buildings had been erected along the eastern edge of St John the Baptist's churchyard by 1721, they remained until the first half of the 20th century; two of the buildings were latterly the Electricity and Waterworks Offices and the Offices of the Borough Surveyor.

Building 3

Pottery evidence from floors and make-up layers associated with the building indicate that it was likely to have been built in the mid-16th century. Its construction almost certainly represents an encroachment on the market place. A well-documented occurrence, the encroachment seems to have taken place from a very early date, firstly by temporary stalls, gradually being replaced by structures of a more permanent nature (Girouard 1990). No earlier structures were identified beneath the make-up layers laid down in advance of construction, although they were likely to have been ephemeral. As is fairly typical of such market place buildings the building appears to have comprised two rows aligned east to west, divided by a narrow lane through the centre. Whether the buildings were constructed as a single enterprise or over a short period of time as separate, but adjoining, premises is unknown. The methods of construction were similar, with the walls made from roughly-worked limestone, but the room sizes varied perhaps suggesting that they were separately constructed shops. The Dean and Chapter, who had control over the market place by this date, would have no doubt levied charges.

Apart from the cloth seal and shears found in the building, there was a significant quantity of window glass; the composition of the assemblage was unusual in that it did not appear to represent the remains of a window smashed during demolition. This suggests the possibility that the glass was instead waste from a glazier. This indicates that a number of different trades were being undertaken on the ground floor of the building, with the traders probably living above the shops. The building may be that shown on the 1610 Speed map of the town. Pottery evidence indicates that it was a relatively short-lived structure, probably demolished by the mid-17th century. Certainly, by 1721, the date of Eyre's map of the city, there was no longer any building in this location.

Street monument: the market cross?

The remains of a structure that had probably been circular or polygonal in plan and *c.*4.5m in diameter, was found to the east of the Guildhall. The most likely structure of this size to be located in the centre of the market place is a market cross. The origins of market crosses are somewhat vague and do not appear to have an entirely religious foundation. Indeed many of them were not even surmounted by a cross, but were simply a pillar during the medieval period. The crosses may have emerged from traditions of creating a relatively safe for trade to occur before there was a central authority to prevent theft or fraud. Market crosses evolved during the later medieval period and post-medieval period into small octagonal buildings, open at the sides. While some were too small for any practical purpose, some were used for the sale of small goods, in particular butter, since it required protection from the sun. Hence, some became known as 'Butter Crosses'.

The base of the monument was constructed from a wide variety of different types of stone, much re-used from other structures, some of it particularly fine. The most likely sources for some of the architectural pieces are the earlier parish church, which was located in Boongate or the nave of St Thomas' Chapel, which occupied a position to the north-west of the cathedral gateway, with its frontage on Long Causeway. This suggests that the monument was constructed in the early 15th century at the same time as the Church of St John the Baptist.

The earliest documentary evidence for a cross seems to be during the reign of King Henry VI in the 15th century, where it is mentioned in a deed, suggesting that the structure found during the excavation may have replaced an even earlier example. It is not known whether this cross was of a simple form comprising a single pillar of stone or whether it was more elaborate. The earliest description of a cross in the market square, in the 16th century, is of a single-storied building, with a roof supported by piers. Butter, poultry and eggs were sold beneath the cross, from which the name of Butter Cross was gained. This structure would appear to be the one over which the 'chamber over the cross was constructed', later known as the Guildhall, in 1671. Speed's map of 1610 appears to show two structures in the eastern half of the market place; possibly the structure found during the excavation as well as the more substantial 'butter cross'. The street monument may have been similar to the 'Butter Cross' at Winchester, which stands on an five-stepped, octagonal base and which is considered to date from the early 15th century.

The graveyard

The discovery of inhumations at the western end of the Church of St John the Baptist was unexpected, since documentary sources had indicated that one had never existed alongside the church, with parishioners being buried on land to the north of the abbey church. In 1477, there is mention of a little garden at the far end of the church (likely to be the eastern end), and in 1534 the Churchwardens were paying for the paving for the churchyard (Tebbs 1979). Butchers Row, thought to be located in the area of the church prior to its construction in the early 15th century, appears to have been built over the graveyard by 1610. The graveyard cannot have been in use prior to the construction of the church or after 1610; it is therefore likely that it was short-lived and probably dated to the earliest use of the church. The graveyard was located *c.* 3m from the west wall of the church and there were at least two rows of intercut burials. It is not known how far west the graveyard extended, since any further burials were truncated by the construction of the Corn Exchange and successive buildings.

There was no definitive evidence of the town ditch in any of the trenches on the eastern side of the market place. The ditch was observed during excavations on Long Causeway, north of the market place. It appears to have defined the western edge of the monastic precinct from the 11th to the 13th centuries and later redefined by a series of ditches and a wall, slightly to the west of the original ditch, probably taking into account a series of tenements along the eastern side of Long Causeway. It was filled in during the 16th/17th centuries. Large ashlar stones, some still mortared together, were observed in one of the trenches in the current excavation and may have been remnants of the bridge that crossed the ditch from the cathedral gateway into the market place. However, the stones were not *in situ*.

Conclusions

Ultimately, the excavations have proved that, while much of the market square has been extensively truncated by former buildings, modern services and remodelling, there is still survival of below-ground archaeological deposits. Many of the interventions observed during the course of this investigation did not penetrate to the earliest archaeological horizons. While this may have limited the analysis of the earliest phases of the development of the market square in this report, it indicates that many of these earliest deposits may remain intact below the level of modern service runs.

However, the excavations have shown that preservation is differential across the site. Perhaps the greatest areas of survival lie in the eastern half, especially to the west of the Cathedral gateway and in those parts of Cathedral Square that remained relatively intact at the deeper levels. Conversely, the archaeological remains along Exchange Street, on the north side of the market and the church, appear to have been almost entirely truncated by significant modern development, and the area of the former butchers' shambles has been largely destroyed by the extensive cellarage of the former Corn Exchange to the west of the church.

There is therefore still great potential for further research into the development of the market square, particularly with regard to pre-market use and subsequently its earliest phases of development, especially since there appears to be scant survival of below-ground remains associated with medieval market places. Ultimately, the repetitive sequence of the build-up of the dark silts and their subsequent burial beneath new surfaces may have served to protect the earliest deposits.

Bibliography

Alexander, J, 1995 Building stone from the east midlands quarries: sources, transportation and usage, *Medieval Archaeol,* **39**, 107-35

Archaeological Services 2008 *Feethams, Darlington Town Centre; Archaeological Desk-based assessment,* Archaeological Services Durham University report

Archaeological Services 2011 *The Market Place, Ripon, North Yorkshire; Post-excavation Analysis,* Archaeological Services Durham University report

Biddle, M, and Smith, D, 1990, Mortars, *in* M Biddle 1990

Biddle, M, 1990 *Object and Economy in Medieval Winchester*, Winchester Studies

Biddle, M, 2005 *Nonsuch Palace, The Material Culture of a Noble Restoration Household*, Oxbow Books

Binford, L, 1978 *Nunamuit Ethnoarchaeology*

Binford, L, 1981 *Bones: Ancient man and modern myth*

Blair, J, 1991 Purbeck Marble, *in* J Blair and N Ramsey (eds) 1991, 41-56

Blair, J, and Ramsey, N, (eds) 1991 *English Medieval Industries,* London

Brothwell, D, and Higgs, E, (eds) 1969 *Science in Archaeology,* London: Thames and Hudson

Brown, N, and Glazebrook, J, 2000 *Research and Archaeology, a Framework for the Eastern Counties, 2 Research agenda and strategy*, East Anglian Archaeol, Occ Pap, **8**

Bull, G, and Payne, S, 1982 Tooth eruption and epiphyseal fusion in pigs and wild boar, *in* B Wilson *et al* (eds) 1982, 55-77

Bull, J, and Bull, V, 2007 *The History of Peterborough Parish Church 1407-2007*

Burke, J, 2008 *Archaeological evaluation at Cathedral Square, Peterborough, November 2008,* Northamptonshire Archaeology report, **08/216**

Cappers, R, Bekker, R, and Jans, J, 2006 *Digital Seed Atlas of the Netherlands,* Barkhuis Publishing, Netherlands

Carus-Wilson, E, 1962 The medieval trade of the ports of the Wash, *Medieval Archaeology,* **6-7**, 182-201

Casa-Hatton, R, Baker, T, and Cooper, S, 2007 *Late Medieval and Post-Medieval remains at the Queensgate Centre and Westgate Arcade, Peterborough,* CAM ARC Report, **958**

Chapman, P, 2008 Ceramic roof tile, *in* P Chapman *et al* 2008, 255-257

Chapman, P, Blinkhorn, P, and Chapman, A, 2008 A medieval potters' tenement at Corby Road, Stanion, *Northamptonshire Archaeol*, **35**, 215-270

Clarke, H, and Carter, A, 1977 *Excavations in King's Lynn, 1963-1970,* Society for Medieval Archaeology, Monog Series, **7**

Cooper, S, and Baker, T, 2003 *Late medieval and post-medieval remains at the Queensgate Centre and Westgate Arcade, Peterborough: Post-excavation assessment,* Cambridgeshire County Council Archaeology Field Unit report, **PXA41**

Cope-Faulkner, P, 2010 *Archaeological monitoring and recording of trial pits at the Market Place, Boston, Lincolnshire*, Archaeological Project Services report

Dallas, C, and Pryor, A M, 1975-6 Peterborough Exchange Street, *Nene Valley Research Committee Annual Report, 1975-76*

Dormer-Harris, M, 1907-13 *The Coventry Leet Book*

Drinkwater, N, 1991 Domestic Stonework, *in* P Saunders and E Saunders (eds) 1991, 169-83

Dunning, G C, 1961, Stone mortars, *in* J G Hurst 1961, 211-99 and 279-84

Dunning, G C, 1977, Mortars, *in* H Clarke and A Carter 1977

EH 1991 *Exploring Our Past,* English Heritage

EH 1997 *English Heritage Archaeology Division Research Agenda,* English Heritage

Egan, G, 1985 *Leaden Cloth Seals*, Finds Research Group Datasheet, **3**

Egan, G, and Pritchard, F, 1991 *Dress Accessories c1150-1450, Medieval Finds from Excavations in London*, **3**, Museum of London

Egan, G, 1991 Lace Chapes, *in* G Egan and F Pritchard 1991, 281-90

Egan, G, 1998 The *Medieval Household, Daily Living c 1150-1450, Medieval Finds from Excavations in London*, **6**, Museum of London

Egan, G, 2005 *Material Culture in London in an Age of Transition: Tudor and Stuart period finds c1450-1700 from excavation at riverside sites in Southwark*, MoLAS monog, **19**

Egan, G, 2005 Lead Objects, *in* M Biddle 2005, 335-358

Ellis, B M A, 1993 Horse Equipment, *in* S Margeson 1993, 220-223

Ellis, P, 2000 *Ludgershall Castle: Excavations by Peter Addyman 1964-1972*, Wiltshire Archaeology and Natural History Society, monog, **2**

Evans, D H, and Tomlinson, D G, 1992 *Excavations at 33-35 Eastgate, Beverley, 1983-86*, Sheffield Excavation Report, **3**

Finch, N, and Jones, A, 2008 *Corn Exchange, Peterborough – Cultural Heritage Assessment,* Scott Wilson

Fletcher, T, and Mould, Q, 2010 Leather-working at the site of Medieval Cumbergate, Peterborough, *Northamptonshire Archaeol*, **36**, 141-152

Foard, G, 1991 The medieval pottery industry of the Rockingham Forest, Northamptonshire, *Medieval Ceramics*, **15**, 13-20

Foreman, M, 1992 Objects of Bone, Antler, and Shell, *in* D H Evans and D G Tomlinson 1992, 163-74

Gardiner, J, with Allen, M J, (ed) 2005 *Before the Mast: Life and Death Aboard the Mary Rose, The Archaeology of the Mary Rose,* **4**, Oxbow Books

Girouard, M, 1990 *The English Town*, Guild Publishing

Glazebrook, J, 1997 *Research and Archaeology, a Framework for the Eastern Counties, 1 Resource Assessment*, East Anglian Archaeol, Occ Pap, **3**

Goubitz, O, 1984 The drawing and registration of archaeological footwear, *Studies in Conservation*, **29**, 187-196

Goubitz, O, van Driel-Murray, C, and Groenman-van Waateringe, W, 2001 *Stepping through Time. Archaeological Footwear from Prehistoric Times until 1800*, Zwolle: StichtingPromotieArcheologie

Greig, J, 1996 Archaeobotanical and historical records compared – a new look at the taphonomy of edible and other useful plants from the 11th to the 18th centuries AD, *Circaea*, **12(2)**, 211-247

Grew, F, and de Neergaard, M, 1988 *Shoes and Pattens. Medieval finds from excavations in London*, **2**, Museum of London

Hall, J, 2004 *Scan of Collection of Loose Stone from Thetford Priory*, unpublished report for English Heritage

Hall, J, 2014 *Emergency Recording of Medieval Architectural Stone at Thorpe Hall, Longthorpe, Peterborough, July-September 2013*, unpublished report

Halstead, P L, 1985 A study of mandibular teeth from Romano-British contexts at Maxey, *in* F Pryor and C French 1985, 219-224

Hurst, J G, 1961 The kitchen area of Northolt Manor, *Medieval Archaeology*, **5**

Hurst, J G, Neal, D S, and Van Beuningen, H J E, 1986 *Pottery produced and traded in north-west Europe, 1350-1650*, Rotterdam Papers, **VI**

IfA 2008a *Standard and guidance for archaeological field evaluation*, Institute for Archaeologists

IfA 2008b *Standard and guidance for an archaeological watching brief*, Institute for Archaeologists

IfA 2008c *Standard and guidance for the collection, documentation, conservation and research of archaeological materials*, Institute for Archaeologists

IfA 2008, revised 2010 *Code of Conduct*, Institute for Archaeologists

Jacomet, S, 2006 *Identification of cereal remains from archaeological sites*, Basel, IPAS

Johnson, G, 1997 The excavation of two Late Medieval kilns with associated buildings at Glapthorn, near Oundle, Northamptonshire, *Medieval Ceramics*, **21**, 13-42

Jones, A E, 1995 *25-26 Long Causeway, Peterborough, Cambridge, Archaeological investigations 1994-1995: A post-excavation assessment and research design*, Birmingham University Field Archaeology Unit report, **317.02**

King, E, 1981 The Town of Peterborough in the early middle Ages, *Northamptonshire Past and Present*, **6(4)**, 187-95

McCarthy, M R, and Brooks, C M, 1988 *Medieval Pottery in Britain AD900-1600*, Leicester University Press

MacGregor, A, Mainman, A J, and Rogers, N S H, 1999 *The Archaeology of York 17/12, Craft, Industry and Everyday Life: Bone, Antler, Ivory and Horn from Anglo-Scandinavian and Medieval York*, York: Council for British Archaeology

Mackreth, D, 1994 *Peterborough, History and a Guide*, Alan Sutton Publishing

Margeson, S, 1993 *Norwich Households: Medieval and Post-medieval Finds from Norwich Survey Excavations 1971-78*, East Anglian Archaeol, **58**

Meadows, I, 1998 *Excavations at the Western Range, Peterborough Cathedral*, Northamptonshire Archaeology report

Meadows, I, 2004 *Archaeological evaluation of 130 Bridge Street, Peterborough, Cambridgeshire 2002-2003*, Northamptonshire Archaeology report

Meadows, I, 2008 A riverside timber revetment at 130 Bridge Street, Peterborough, *Northamptonshire Archaeol*, **35**, 163-172

Mellows, W T, 1937 *Peterborough Local Administration: Parochial Government from the Reformation to the Revolution 1541-1689 being Minutes and Accounts of the Feoffees and the Governors of the City Lands*, Northampton Record Society, **X**

Mellows, W T, (ed) 1939 *Peterborough Local Administration: Churchwardens Accounts 1467-1573, Supplementary Documents 1107-1488*, Northampton Record Society, **IX**

Mellows, W T, 1947 *The last days of Peterborough Monastery*, Northamptonshire Record Society, **XII**

Mellows, W T, and Gifford, H, 1956 *Elizabethan Peterborough: The Dean and Chapter as Lords of the City*, Northampton Record Society, **XVIII**

Morris, S, and Yates, A, 2012 *Assessment report and Updated Project Design: An archaeological investigation of the historical development of Cathedral Square, Peterborough, November 2008 to August 2011*, Northamptonshire Archaeological report, **12/48**

Morris, S, 2016 *An archaeological investigation of the historical development of Cathedral Square, Peterborough: November 2008 to August 2011*, MOLA Northampton report, **16/105**

Mould, Q, and Cameron, E, 2005 Leather buckets, *in* J Gardiner, with M J Allen (ed) 2005, 359-367

Mould, Q, 1995 *Assessment of Leather from 25/26 Long Causeway, Peterborough, Cambridgeshire (LCW95)*, typescript submitted to The Field Archaeology Unit University of Birmingham June 1995

Mould, Q, 2006 *The Leather from Queensgate, Peterborough (PET QC01)*, typescript submitted to the Archaeological Field Unit, Cambridgeshire County Council, June 2006

Mould, Q. (2009) *The Leather from the Grand Arcade, Cambridge*, typescript submitted to Cambridge Archaeological Unit, February 2009

NA 2006 *Archaeological Fieldwork Manual*, Northamptonshire Archaeology

NA 2009 *Public Realm Works Cathedral Square, St John's Square, Cumbergate, Exchange Street And Church Street, Peterborough, Specification For Archaeological Works*, Northamptonshire Archaeology

O'Neill, F, 1978 Excavations at Bridge Street, Peterborough, *Durobrivae*, **6**, 30-31

Ottaway, P, and Rogers, N, 2002 *Craft, Industry and Everyday Life: Finds from Medieval York,* York

Payne, S, 1973 Kill-off patterns in Sheep and goats: the mandibles from Asvan Kale, *Anatolian Studies,* **23**, 281-303

Pritchard, F, 1991, Strap-ends, *in* G Egan and F Pritchard 1991, 124-161

Pryor, F, and French, C, 1985 *The Fenland Project No 1 Archaeology and environment in the Lower Welland Valley,* East Anglian Archaeol, **27**

Pryor, A M, 1977-8 Peterborough Queensgate Centre (TL 1913 9873), *Nene Valley Research Committee Annual Report,* 1977-8

RCHME 1969 *Archaeological Survey of Peterborough New Town,* Royal Commission on Historical Monuments, England, HMSO

Raban, S, (ed) 2001 *The White Book of Peterborough: Registers of Abbott William of Woodford 1295-99 and Abbott Geoffrey of Crowland 1299-1321,* Northamptonshire Record Society

Robinson, B, and Casa-Hatton, R, 2009 *Brief for Archaeological Investigation, The Norwich Union Building (Corn Exchange) demolition and associated public realm of works, Peterborough city centre,* Peterborough City Council Archaeological Service, Peterborough Museum and Art Gallery

Robinson, P, and Griffiths, N, 2000 The Copper alloy Objects, *in* B M A Ellis 2000, 124-137

Rylatt, M, and Mason, P, 2003 *The archaeology of the medieval Cathedral and Priory of St Mary, Coventry,* Coventry City Council/Millennium Commission

Saunders, P, and Saunders, E, (eds) 1991 *Salisbury Museum Medieval Catalogue,* **1**, Salisbury

Schoch, W H, Pawlik, B, and Schweingruber, F H, 1988 *Botanical macro-remains,* Berne, Paul Haupt

Silver, I, 1969 The ageing of domestic mammals, *in* D Brothwell and E Higgs 1969

Soden, I, 2005/2013 *Coventry: The Hidden History,* Tempus, The History Press

Spoerry, P, and Hinman, M, 1998 *The Still, Peterborough: medieval remains between Cumbergate and Westgate,* Cambridgeshire Archaeological Field Unit, monog, **1**

Sutherland, D, 2003 *Northamptonshire Stone,* Dovecote Press

Tebbs, H F, 1997*Peterborough, A History,* Oleander Press

Von den Driesch, A, 1976 *Guide to the measurement of animal bones from Archaeological sites,* Harvard: University Press

Walker, C, 2010 *Archaeological watching brief at the Church of St John the Baptist, Peterborough,* Northamptonshire Archaeology report, **10/89**

Ward-Perkins, J B, 1993 *London Museum Medieval catalogue 1940,* Anglia publishing (reprinted 1993)

Watson, J P N, 1979 The estimation of the relative frequencies of mammalian species: Khirokitia, *Journal of Archaeological Science,* **6**, 127-37

Welsh, K, 1994 *The Still, Peterborough, medieval deposits behind Cumbergate and Westgate,* Cambridgeshire County Council Archaeological Field Unit report, **101**

Wilson, B, Grigson, C, and Payne, S, (eds) 1982 *Ageing and sexing animal bones from archaeological sites,* British Archaeological Reports, British Series, **109**, Oxford

VCH 1936 *A History of the County of Huntingdon,* **3**, Victoria County History

Websites

Geology: http://www.bgs.ac.uk/geoindex/index.htm
Charred seeds: http://www.asis.scri.ac.uk